"Edie Melson provides parents with p[...] [...] needful encouragement. I'm plannin[...] [...] nightstand!"

—**James Watkins**, award-winning author of books for teens and their parents, author of *The Imitation of Christ: Classic Devotions in Today's Language*

"You will be delighted with Edie Melson's new book *While My Child Is Away*. I so identify with the heart of these prayers and am grateful for others who put into words that which often escapes me."

—**Lucinda Secrest McDowell**, author of *Dwelling Places*, EncouragingWords.net

"*While My Child is Away* is a literary treasure chest for parents, overflowing with prayers, devotions, Scripture verses, quotes, and personal applications. Written with author Edie Melson's appealing honesty, this book will strengthen parents' prayer lives and improve their relationships with their children."

—**Beth K. Vogt**, 2016 Christy Award finalist, author of *Almost Like Being in Love*

"In *While My Child is Away*, Edie Melson helps us find comfort by taking fears to the Speaker of Peace, the One who sees all, knows all, and loves our children more than we do."

—**Vonda Skelton**, speaker and author, Founder Christian Communicators

"In one swift movement, Edie Melson has pulled the heart back into our prayer life by praying, simplistic, heartfelt, naked prayers before the Lord God Almighty, who simply wishes for us to bring our needs and desires before Him."

—**Cindy Sproles,** best-selling author of *Mercy's Rain*, executive editor and cofounder, Christian Devotions

While My Child Is Away

My Prayers for
When We Are Apart

Edie Melson

WORTHY℠
Inspired

Published by Worthy Inspired, an imprint of Worthy Publishing Group, a division of Worthy Media, Inc., One Franklin Park, 6100 Tower Circle, Suite 210, Franklin, TN 37067.

WORTHY is a registered trademark of Worthy Media, Inc.

HELPING PEOPLE EXPERIENCE THE HEART OF GOD

Library of Congress Cataloging-in-Publication Data

Names: Melson, Edie, author.
Title: While my child is away : my prayers for when we are apart / Edie
  Melson.
Description: Franklin, TN : Worthy Inspired, an imprint of Worthy Publishing
  Group, a division of Worthy Media, Inc., [2016]
Identifiers: LCCN 2016012926 | ISBN 9781617957314 (tradepaper)
Subjects: LCSH: Parents--Religious life. | Intercessory prayer--Christianity.
  | Prayers.
Classification: LCC BV4529 .M425 2016 | DDC 242/.845--dc23
LC record available at http://lccn.loc.gov/2016012926

ISBN: 978-1-61795-731-4

For foreign and subsidiary rights, contact rights@worthypublishing.com

Cover Design: Jeff Jensen / Aesthetic Soup

Printed in the United States of America

16 17 18 19 20 21 LBM 10 9 8 7 6 5 4 3 2 1

This book is gratefully dedicated to
my three sons:

John Melson
Kirk E. Melson
Jimmy Melson

I couldn't be more proud of the amazing
young men you've become.
Thank you for putting up with
and actually encouraging
your eccentric Mom!

Contents

Foreword   ix

Introduction   1

How to Use this Book   2

1. The Triumph of Love   3

2. Making Good Choices   29

3. Peace Beyond Circumstances   53

4. True Self-Confidence   77

5. A Foundation of Faith   101

6. A Core of Strength   127

7. Companions Matter   153

8. My God, My Defender   179

9. Fully Present   203

Acknowledgments   225

Foreword

Michelle Medlock Adams

I normally start my day with prayer but I was running late for my sister's Bible study that particular morning, so I skipped my regular prayer time, grabbed a breakfast bar and a Diet Coke, and hurried out the door. Just as I was pulling out of the driveway, I felt a real urgency to pray for my college-age daughters. With the three-hour time difference between Indiana and California, I knew Ally wasn't even up yet, but Abby was already headed to Kentucky to see her boyfriend pitch in a college baseball tournament. I prayed Psalm 91 over Ally and Abby and thanked God that their guardian angels were watching over them. I continued praying and praising God for my precious daughters until I felt a peace come over me. Then I went ahead into Bible study, walking in only a few minutes late.

Moments later, my phone vibrated. Just as I was about to turn off my phone, I saw the call was from Abby so I excused myself and answered.

"Mom," she said, through sobs.

"What's wrong?"

"I was just almost in an accident . . ."

After hearing those words, my heart was pounding so hard that I thought it would escape my chest. Abby went on to explain what had happened to her.

A car had pulled out of the median, almost sideswiping her, causing her to swerve into the right lane to avoid contact. Before the incident was over, her car and three others were off the road, and Abby's vehicle had spun completely around.

"Mom, I don't even know how that car missed me," she kept saying. "I saw it coming right at me!"

I knew.

"Because at the exact time this happened to you, Ab, God prompted me to pray for you," I shared. "I was praying Psalm 91 over you and thanking God that your guardian angels were watching over you this morning!"

We both cried and praised the Lord and rejoiced that this was only an "almost accident." People who aren't Christians might write this off as a "mother's intuition," but we know better, don't we? It was God who caused me to pray at the exact time that Abby was coming up on that crazy driver, and it was God who miraculously moved her little VW Bug out of harm's way.

As mothers, we are that first line of prayer defense when it comes to our kiddos. With everything we do for our children— from being their taxi drivers to fixing their meals to doing their laundry to helping them with homework—nothing is more important than covering them with prayer.

No one knows this truth better than my friend, colleague, and sister-in-Christ, Edie Melson. I've seen her stand for her sons as they battled heartbreaks and physical ailments. I've seen her go to God for protection over her son who bravely served in our military. I've seen her pray diligently that her sons would walk in their callings, find their soul mates, and serve God every day of their lives.

And I've seen those prayers answered.

Edie is one of my favorite friends. She's Southern, charming, gifted, accomplished, caring, and funny. But she's also a serious prayer warrior who has put in the "knee time" for her children, and I have always admired her the most for that attribute. Though

I have two daughters and she has three sons, we've been able to share parenting advice with one another. We've laughed together. We've cried together. But more than anything, we've prayed.

For each other.

And for our children.

And when praying mamas hit their knees, the devil gets nervous.

This book might just give the devil a nervous breakdown. Seriously, it will be your go-to resource when you don't know what to pray for your children, but you know that you should. From praying that your son will make good choices to praying that your daughter will feel valued and stay pure, this book covers it all and feels very personal. As I read Edie's prayers, I thought, *That's just what I would have wanted to pray when my youngest daughter moved to Los Angeles to follow her dream of attending the Fashion Institute of Design & Merchandising.*

I also loved the prayers for us—the parents—that are included in each chapter. And the heartfelt devotions in each section so beautifully drive home the focus of each topical chapter, giving us a glimpse into Edie's own parenting triumphs and even a few mishaps. Her transparency is refreshing and made me love her even more.

Even though you may not know Edie like I do, as you go through this book, you'll feel like she's your best buddy, and you'll welcome her as your prayer partner.

One of my favorite passages from this book is in the section called "Always Pray First":

As my kids spent more and more time away from home, it became more and more important. I start my day with prayer, my meals with prayer, and every single parenting decision with prayer.

Sometimes the prayers are more in the vein of distress flares shot toward heaven, but it's the fact I'm praying that's important. It gives me confidence to be reminded that I'm not in this alone and I'm not the ultimate authority.

The prayer for my daughter Abby that morning was more of a distress flare, though I didn't know it at the time. But it's like Edie writes—it's the fact that I prayed that was important. We don't have to be all-knowing, because we serve a God who is, and as Edie reminded me, I'm not in this parenting thing alone.

And neither are you.

God has given us precious treasures to take care of, watch over, protect, and love. And though we're not always going to get it right, because we're human, we have the privilege of praying to our Heavenly Father, who is perfect and who loves our children even more than we do.

Now that my girls are officially "out of the nest," I am very aware that I can't always be there physically when they need me, but I can pray from wherever I am and know that God is on the job. He never slumbers. He's never late. He's in control. And He hears my prayers.

He'll hear your prayers, too—even the ones your heart utters when you have no words.

Let this book guide you into a deeper, more targeted, more powerful prayer life where your children are concerned.

There's no greater gift you could give them.

Introduction

Three days after I signed the contract for this book, two of my sons went for an afternoon kayak trip on a nearby river. They are fully grown and capable young men—one served in the military and the other has a degree in outdoor leadership. They're both married, are *not* novices about the outdoors or about life in general. As experienced outdoorsmen, they don't ever take unnecessary chances. So the confidence I have in their ability isn't misplaced. Even with that, I felt a momentary battle of *what-if* when they told me about their proposed outing. Instead of voicing my fears, I told them to have fun and took my motherly worries to the One who can ensure their safety.

The next day I found out just how close I'd come to losing both sons.

They'd been on the river when a strong thunderstorm moved in with unusual speed. Immediately they headed to shore, but never made it to safety. They woke up three and a half hours later. Both were in the river, separated from their boats and each other. One son was caught on a snag in the middle of the river, the other was lying half-in and half-out of the water on the shore. After they'd found each other—a harrowing ten minutes later, they'd assured me—they assessed the injuries they'd sustained and realized they'd been struck by lightning.

While both are fine, with no lasting damage, this once again reinforced the fact that we never know when our children are headed into a dangerous situation. Whether our kids are headed to first grade, camp, college, or just a day at play, we need to be praying for them. Not just general, "God, please protect my child" prayers, either. We need to invest in a solid set of knee pads and be ready to do battle for them on a daily basis.

That's what this book is about.

Any time our children are away from us can be a time of anxiety. We can't always help the emotions that accompany specific situations, but we can *always* take those emotions to the One who will provide the protection they need and the peace we crave.

How to Use This Book

This book is divided into chapters, based on the topics parents would want to pray for their children. The individual prayers cover a multitude of situations, from a child away for the day at school, traveling for a short trip, off to college, or having left home for another reason. Because of the different topics covered, the prayers span a fairly large age range of the children being prayed for.

Within each chapter, there is a section of prayers that parents would pray for their children, followed by a section that a parent might pray for themselves. Following these two divisions, each chapter also contains a section of devotions about parenting. Finally there is a small section at the end of each chapter with parenting thoughts pertaining to the chapter's topic.

This book can be used individually or as a resource for a group of parents who have banded together to pray for one another's children.

Chapter One

The Triumph of Love

We all want our children to feel love—from us and especially from God. But it's hard when we're not close enough physically to ensure our kids get the attention we think they need.

Make Your Love Real in My Child's Life

We love the things we love for what they are.

Robert Frost

Dear Lord, I know You love my child in ways that I never can. But it's so hard to be away from her, now that she's growing up. She and I used to spend so much time together, and I was always the one she turned to first. Now that she's away more, I'm afraid that if I'm not with her, she won't have anyone near to reassure her that she is loved.

I don't want to be replaced in her life, but even more than that, I don't want her to be alone. Don't let her feel abandoned, or mistake physical distance for emotional distance. Help her remember how much I love her. Put people around her who will show her love in ways that help her feel connected. Make sure she remembers that no matter what, You love her with an eternal and infinite love. Give her a foundation of Your love that will never be shaken.

You are the Author of love. Help her discover the depth of Your love, and give her opportunities to share that with those around her. Wrap Your love around her and be all that she needs. Amen.

I love those who love me and those who seek me find me.

Proverbs 8:17 niv

Redefine Love in My Child's Life

God loves each of us as if there were only one of us.

AUGUSTUS

Dear Lord, I know the Bible tells us that You are love. But even with that, our human understanding is so limited. Right now, my child is struggling to define what real love is. I'm asking You to use this time to give him Your definition of love.

Show him all the ways it goes beyond emotions. Help him see that it even goes beyond tolerance and acceptance. Let him see the physical manifestation of godly love in his life and in the lives of those around him. Give him examples of the miracles found within tough love. In his situation today, love has limits. Let him experience the limitlessness of Your perfect love.

Help him replace all the incorrect definitions he believes with Your truth. Our kids are exposed to so many twisted examples of love. Protect his mind, from this day forward, from anything that isn't from You. Bring him back to the basics. Erase the things that aren't truth and use those near him to reinforce Your truth.

Surround him with people who know Your love and are willing to share Your truth with him. Give them the words to speak that will resonate in his soul. Most of all, let it shine in their lives as they become real-life examples of You. Amen.

Give thanks to the God of heaven! His love is eternal.
PSALM 136:26 HCSB

Thank You for Loving My Child

Though our feelings come and go, God's love for us does not.
C. S. LEWIS

Dear Lord, as grateful as I am for Your love in my life, I'm even more thankful for the fact that You love my child. You have proven trustworthy in my life, and I know I can trust You with my child.

I admit I'm scared that she's away from home more now. This isn't just a time of growth for her, but it is also a time of growth for me. I'm having to draw on all my reserves to get through this. I know other parents experience this, but somehow when I watched it didn't seem as hard for them.

Lord, I'm thankful that my child knows You and has already come to rely on You. You have shown her love in so many ways during her life. Neither one of us could ever doubt how much You care for her.

I'm asking that You remind us both of Your love. We're sad to be apart, even though this is an exciting time of growth. I didn't realize how much comfort I drew daily from having her close by, and now she's miles away. I can hear her voice on the phone, but it's not the same.

I'm learning to trust You, Lord, in a whole new way. Thank You for the assurances You've already given me. Be with us both as we adjust to life's new normal. Amen.

We love because he first loved us.
1 JOHN 4:19 NIV

Remind My Child That You Are Jealous for His Love

Remember, you are special because I made you.
And I don't make mistakes.

MAX LUCADO

Dear Lord, You love us so much. The Bible tells us You are jealous for us. In our culture today, we view jealousy in a negative way. But I know how unbelievably precious it is to know that You, God, are jealous for me. Make this truth real in my child's life. Give him a new and deeper perspective of Your love through this aspect of Your character.

So often, in the activities and busyness of life we forget that spending time with You isn't just for our benefit; it's because You love us. Your love has a depth that we can't ever completely understand. But the more time we spend with You, the more we begin to understand Your love.

Give him insight into who You are and let that fuel his hunger for You. Reinforce that drive through the companions who surround him.

Put an unquenchable desire to spend time with You in my child's heart. Teach him how much You want his company. You want to be the center of all our lives. Make Yourself the center of my child's life. Amen.

"Do not worship any other god, for the LORD, whose name is Jealous, is a jealous God."

EXODUS 34:14 NIV

Teach My Child
Your Love Never Fails

No matter what storm you face, you need to know
that God loves you. He has not abandoned you.

Franklin Graham

Dear Lord, I know that Your love is constant and never failing. Help my child to know and acknowledge this. When something difficult happens, help him to turn to You.

When his circumstances are difficult, and he's away from all that's familiar, help him to see beyond his situation. Show him how You are working in his life right now.

Give him wise mentors and companions who can see beyond what's happening in the moment and help him. Use them to redirect his eyes upward. Lead him to see how Your love is shepherding him through this experience.

Let him catch a glimpse of how challenges now, will be used for good later on—not just in his life, but in the lives of others. Allow him to see how wide-reaching Your love is. You are in the details of right now, and he needs to experience this.

Surround him with others whose lives can give him proof of how Your love is always enough, and always on time. As they open up to my child, give him the insight to see You at work. Amen.

May the Lord direct your hearts to God's love and Christ's endurance.

2 Thessalonians 3:5 hcsb

Show My Child Love's Discipline

God has no pleasure in afflicting us, but He will not
keep back even the most painful chastisement
if He can but thereby guide His beloved child
to come home and abide in the beloved Child.

ANDREW MURRAY

Dear Lord, when my child is facing difficult challenges—and I'm not there to remind him—show him that he's not alone and that others are not against him.

Even if he has made some choices that have led him into a tough situation, help him to face it, knowing that You are by his side. Give him insight into what to do next. Don't let these situations make him angry and bitter. Show him that the people holding him accountable are doing it out of love for him.

Remind him that we only care about his actions because we care about him. Use his friends to encourage him during these difficult times. Bring others into his life who've had similar experiences and learned from them.

Most of all, don't let him turn away from You. Being held accountable is hard, but help him see he's going to come out of this stronger. Teach him the lessons he needs to learn gently, but firmly, and never let him feel abandoned. Amen.

*For whom the LORD loves
He reproves, even as a father
corrects the son in whom
he delights.*

PROVERBS 3:12 NASB

Show My Child How Much I Love Him

I love to think of nature as an unlimited broadcasting station,
through which God speaks to us every hour,
if we will only tune in.

GEORGE WASHINGTON CARVER

Dear Lord, when my child is far from home, please remind him how much I love him. When we talk, help us to be as close as if we were together. Never let him forget how much I love him.

Remind him of all the times I've shown him my love. Help us both to understand this situation and find a way for us to talk to one another.

Sometimes things happen that are beyond our control. Help me to understand how he feels. Please intervene on my behalf. Put people in his life who will help him remember the proof of my love and care. Help us to find our way back to one another.

Lord, please put people in both of our lives who can speak truths that we need to hear. Help us not to focus on what has taken us away from each other, but instead focus on You. Give him Your perspective and concrete proof of my love. Amen.

Hatred stirs up conflicts, but love covers all offenses.

PROVERBS 10:12 HCSB

Show My Child the Power of Love

I have found that there are three stages in every
great work of God: first, it is impossible,
then it is difficult, then it is done.

JAMES HUDSON TAYLOR

Dear Lord, please protect my child from bullies and false friends
who say hurtful things and call it "joking." I know it's got to be
tempting to lash back with angry words, but I'm asking You to
help him return love instead of hate.

I don't know how I'd react in similar circumstances. But
looking from the outside in, I can see how You'd expect me to
react. So far that's exactly what my child is doing. I'm so proud
of the way he's handled this. It's beginning to take its toll on him,
though.

As he shows only love toward the people ridiculing him, I
pray that You show him the power of that love. I've seen Your
love bring hope where there is no hope, redeem a situation beyond redemption, and even change
a person from hopeless to joyful. I
want my child to see that kind of
transformation here.

Even if transformation isn't
part of Your plan, I'm asking that
You show Yourself to my child in
a new way. Let him see the purpose
behind this experience. Make sure
He can feel Your pride in the way
he's handling himself. Amen.

*It was not by their sword that
they won the land, nor did
their arm bring them victory;
it was your right hand, your
arm, and the light of your
face, for you loved them.*

PSALM 44:3 NIV

Restore My Relationship with My Child

Love is an act of endless forgiveness.

JEAN VANIER

Dear Lord, my child and I are separated by so much more than just distance. As hard as it is to be away from him physically, it's even harder to bear the distance that has developed in our relationship. We've let our differences build a wall between us and it breaks my heart.

Show me how to reconnect with him. Give him a forgiving heart toward me, and me to him. Help us look past the hurts and move forward toward reconciliation.

It hurts me to see him making decisions that I know will affect him in years to come. Help me show him how much I love him even when I disagree. Don't let him believe that my disapproval affects the love I have for him.

As I begin doing my part to repair our relationship, urge him to meet me halfway. Surround him with people who will help us find our way back to each other. Show us both where we have common ground. Most of all, speak to his heart and draw him close to You. Amen.

Therefore, my dear brothers and sisters, stand firm. Let nothing move you. Always give yourselves fully to the work of the Lord, because you know that your labor in the Lord is not in vain.

1 CORINTHIANS 15:58 NIV

Make Me a Good Example of Your Love

I used to ask God to help me. Then I asked if I might help Him.
I ended up by asking Him to do His work through me.

JAMES HUDSON TAYLOR

Dear Lord, I don't know where I'd be without Your love. Even now, in the midst of this time apart from my child, I feel You with me. I want to do more than just feel Your love. I want to share it with others. I want You to work through me and make me an example of Your love.

There are so many challenges right now with my child being away from home more and more. I want to do more than just endure. I want to have a positive impact.

I know the best way to do that is to show Your love to all those involved. Even when it is hard or I don't like the reason we are apart or I don't like the people in my child's life, show me how to be a beacon of love.

You've given me the capacity to love them, but my emotions don't appear to know that. Help me show Your love to everyone, no matter what my feelings toward them are. Most of all, use my life to illustrate how much You love each of us. Show others the way You guide and protect all of us who call You Lord. Amen.

I will instruct you and teach you in the way you should go; I will counsel you with my loving eye on you.

PSALM 32:8 NIV

Help Me Love Those My Child Is With

Love is always open arms. If you close your arms about love,
you will find that you are left holding only yourself.

LEO BUSCAGLIA

Dear Lord, I want my child home with me. I know he's where he's supposed to be right now, but it's hard. He has new people in his life, and when I talk to him I feel left out. I am happy that he seems so happy when I talk to him, but it hurts because I'm unhappy that he is away. Help me replace my resentment with love.

In my head, I know I haven't been replaced. But my heart feels otherwise. I don't want to like those people, much less love them. Yet if my child loves them, there's got to be some good in them. He's not unwise when it comes to judging character.

Show me how to move past my feelings of hurt and learn to love those he's with right now. We all want the best for him, that I do know. Even more than that, I trust You, God. You love him more than I do, and I have to accept that You are still in control of the situation.

Give me more reasons to love these people. Help me see the good in them. Let me see examples of how they're good for my child, and they're working with me to help him grow up. Open my eyes to see them with Your love instead of my own fears. Amen.

"I give you a new command: Love one another. Just as I have loved you, you must also love one another."

JOHN 13:34 HCSB

Open My Eyes to Others in the Same Situation as Me

I want the love that cannot help but love;
Loving, like God, for the very sake of love.

A. B. SIMPSON

Dear Lord, I'm so sad right now. I miss my child and wish she was back home with me. She's moving on and into an exciting part of her life, but it's still hard not to have her here every day. I know I've got to take the focus off of what's happening in my life, otherwise I'll drown in these circumstances. Help me to reach out to others who are in similar circumstances.

There are other parents dealing with the same things I am, I'm sure of it. Help me look beyond myself and find them. Give me others to care for and love on.

I'm not very far down this path, but I'm willing to walk it with others who are hurting. Show me how I can find others who feel the same way I do. Open my eyes to see them when they pass through my daily comings and goings.

Don't let me become so self-absorbed that I miss the opportunity to share Your love with those I encounter. Give me insight to know whom You'd have me reach out to. Use this situation to stretch me and teach me more about You. Show me how I can love those who are also hurting. Amen.

Be devoted to one another in love. Honor one another above yourselves.
ROMANS 12:10 NIV

Accepting Love on Their Terms

> *Dear children, let us not love with words or speech*
> *but with actions and in truth.*
> 1 JOHN 3:18 NIV

There are certain things that mean a lot to me as a mom. One of them is getting to sit in church with all my boys. I love being able to come together to worship. Although I don't like to admit it, I am proud that none of my kids are ashamed to sit with me. It makes me feel special. But I didn't realize how important that was to me until one particular Mother's Day.

It was 2006 and the last Mother's Day we'd all be together for a while because our oldest child had enlisted in the military. I was already frustrated that morning because my husband was out of town on a business trip. All I could think of was that this was my holiday and he'd chosen to travel. Because of that, I was placing even more emphasis on the fact that all three boys would be with me in church.

The boys hadn't left from home at the same time as me, so I made my way into the sanctuary and saved them room on the pew beside me. I hated doing that, especially on such a busy Sunday, but I really wanted to be able to sit with them. I waited and waited, finally giving up the empty seats and fumed my way through the service.

By the time I got home I was loaded and ready to explode all over them. It was my special day and they couldn't be bothered to show up. Didn't they even love me? Tears warred with anger as I let my hurt take control.

As I got out of the car, I noticed something odd. There were flower petals all over the sidewalk that led to the back of the house and onto the screened porch. It was odd because we didn't have those types of flowers blooming and they hadn't been there when I'd left just a couple of hours earlier. Curious, I decided to see what was up. I followed the trail and heard laughter. I opened the porch door and was met with three smiling faces and the beautiful aroma of fresh flowers. There on the porch floor, spelled out in fresh petals were the words, *We Love You!*

In an effort to show how much they really did love me and still be original, they'd spent the morning collecting the petals and arranging them in a message. Of course my anger evaporated instantly as I felt their love envelop me.

They taught me something valuable that day and it's stayed with me. I've learned to accept their love in the way they offer it, without judging or expectations. This is especially important when they're away from home. It's easy to misunderstand intentions and feel neglected. I let this example stay strong as I remember they show their love in many different ways. God's love doesn't always come in ways we expect, but that lesson has helped me find love in places and ways I never imagined.

How Looks Can Be Deceiving

> *And He will delight in the fear of the* LORD,
> *And He will not judge by what His eyes see,*
> *Nor make a decision by what His ears hear.*
>
> ISAIAH 11:3 NASB

Our middle child has always seemed to be the one who chose to learn things the hard way. One of his hardest lessons came when he was a new camp counselor. When he began his training with other new hires, one of the things emphasized was the safety of the campers who'd be in their charge. There were hours of procedures they had to memorize, first aid classes they had to take, and exams they had to pass. He came through with flying colors—at least in the head knowledge part of the education.

To celebrate, the counselors were released to spend a weekend hiking and camping in the nearby mountains. About midway through the second day, they were halfway up a fairly steep hike and his canteen ran dry. Instead of accepting water from someone else, he decided the nearby stream would be a perfect solution to his dilemma. He inspected the area, saw that the water ran clear, and decided to slake his thirst—in spite of the fact that he'd just spent weeks in classes warning them against this very thing.

Sure enough, within twenty-four hours the cramping, nausea, and other symptoms began. Thinking it would pass, he tried to push through. When it didn't, he went to the camp nurse. As she questioned him about his recent actions, she hit on the water in the stream as the cause. Several blood tests confirmed he'd gotten a nasty parasite from that "sparkling clean" brook.

It was a hard lesson, but my child now understands how deceiving looks can be. It was also a difficult lesson to me. I already worry when my kids are out of my sight, and at first glance this seemed to justify my fears. But studying the situation more, I see that it's a confirmation of God's faithfulness. He has lessons for each of us—even our kids—and we don't always need to be there to make sure they get the point.

Our child has shared that well-learned lesson with the boys he's led, using it to illustrate a spiritual truth that's become foundational in his life.

A Stone's Throw from Grace

> *When they kept on questioning him, he straightened up*
> *and said to them, "Let any one of you who is without sin*
> *be the first to throw a stone at her."*
>
> JOHN 8:7 NIV

Imagine with me the scene that day. A woman has been caught in the act of adultery. In biblical times, it's a crime punishable by death—death by stoning. The men and women drag her into the public square. I can hear the voices of her accusers, raised in hatred and condemnation.

"You're nothing but filth."

"You knew what could happen when you made your choice."

"Get rid of her. We can't have someone like her contaminating our town."

She's thrown at the feet of a famous teacher, for Him to pronounce the death sentence. Why did they bring her to Him? Because He's known for His compassion. By bringing her crime to His attention, they can literally kill two birds with one stone. They can get rid of a sinner and expose Him as either a liar or a lawbreaker.

Instead, Jesus introduces them all to the concept of grace. He does it without compromising the law or the heart of compassion He's known for.

Back in the viewpoint of our sinner, I can imagine her lying there at His feet, covering her head with her arms as she tries to make herself as small a target as possible. Every muscle is tensed, waiting for the first stone from the angry mob.

As the crowd begins to quiet, instead of the sound of stones whistling through the air, she hears the words of the teacher. His pronouncement takes them all by surprise—even her. I can imagine that the next sounds she hears are the *thumps* all around her as the stones drop to the ground, before the crowd disperses.

Those in the crowd learned as valuable a lesson as did the woman. They learned that they have a choice when it comes to confronting sin. They can be stone-throwers or stone-droppers.

I realized that I've been guilty of throwing a few stones in my life too—especially when it comes to judging other parents. Although a different parenting style doesn't necessarily equate to sin, it's still easy to throw stones today at others who choose to do things another way. This is especially true when our kids are away from us, interacting with those other parents.

But the truth is, different kids need different parents and different approaches. Other styles of parenting don't mean that one is acting in sin and another isn't. Only God knows the truth of each situation. As I interact with others raising kids, I find I still have a choice today. I can heave a stone at someone who's handling things differently or extend grace. I'm choosing to drop the stones.

Damage Control

No discipline seems enjoyable at the time, but painful.
Later on, however, it yields the fruit of peace and
righteousness to those who have been trained by it.

HEBREWS 12:11 HCSB

We recently found ourselves in the middle of some minor household renovations. It didn't start because we planned to update a room. It began because of a small problem. We had a small leak in one of the pipes behind our commode. It was so small it seemed more of an irritation than an actual problem.

Wrong.

By the time we got around to dealing with it, the damage was extensive. Fortunately our child has worked in construction, and he was able to do the work for us. But it meant he had to cut out several large sections of Sheetrock and replace it. Other than the time, as well as the money, there was also the mess and general disruption to our lives.

First, he had to get to the damage, and that meant emptying the room. Then he had to cut out the damage, and replace the parts that were ruined. Finally, he had to spend a *lot* of time sanding to get the old and new to fit back together. I had no idea sanding could cause so much dust and mess.

As I watched him fix the mess we'd made by ignoring a small leak, I couldn't help but draw the parallel between that and our spiritual lives.

So often we tend to ignore the small things that creep into the lives of our kids when they're here with us. It's hard to be the bad guy sometimes, especially when the infraction is small and we're all tired. They don't seem to be big enough to bother anyone or cause any damage, so we just let them go. But things can quickly multiply, especially when our kids are away from home more and more. By the time we realize the damage, we can have a big mess on our hands. A mess that's too big to handle alone.

That's where prayer comes in. Going to Jesus for help is a lot like us going to our child for the bathroom repair. Jesus loves us and stands ready to help. Just like our child did, He has the ability and authority to get us back in shape. Time and distance are nothing to Him, so I've learned that when the cracks appear, it's time to hit my knees and call in the Master Carpenter.

Too Close

Frogs seemed to be a recurring theme in the early years of parenting. I'm not particularly squeamish, but they're not an animal I'm fond of. My boys, on the other hand, were fascinated by these lumpy, slimy amphibians.

One day, at the end of a hard day of laundry and mothering, I was moving the last load from washer to dryer. I wasn't paying attention, and when my hand encountered something unusual, instead of dropping it, I pulled it into the light for closer inspection.

The boys say the scream could be heard two houses in any direction.

In my hand was the limp remains of a medium-sized frog. After regaining my composure, I eyed the three small faces staring at me from the doorway. I already had an idea of which one had been the culprit, but I needed to be certain.

"Who decided a frog in the laundry was a good idea?"

The youngest giggled, and the oldest rolled his eyes, while our middle child crossed his arms and glared, his seven-year-old frame radiating outrage. Obviously there was more to this story than I'd thought. I dismissed the other two and pulled the offended child into my lap. "Want to tell me what happened?"

"Did you kill my frog?" He sniffed and rubbed a grimy hand across his eyes.

"Not on purpose." I gave him a squeeze. "Where was he?"

"I wanted to keep him safe, so I put him in my pocket." Tears welled up in his eyes. "I guess I forgot to take him out."

I took time to comfort him, and pretty soon he was back outside playing.

I, on the other hand, couldn't get the incident out of my mind. Was I like my child, keeping my kids tucked safely away in my pocket? Perhaps that wasn't as safe a place as I'd envisioned. Was God reminding me that as they grew, I'd have to let them out in the big, scary world? It wasn't something I wanted to do, but I knew it was something I needed to do.

MODEL GOD'S LOVE THROUGH YOUR PARENTING.

As a parent, I was a tempted to present myself as someone who had already arrived. I felt more credible and more of an authority if I had everything right.

The truth is really the exact opposite.

I found I didn't have to be perfect to be a role model. My kids responded better when I dropped the mask and became real.

If I messed up, I went to them and admitted it and asked for forgiveness. If I was struggling with someone or something, I would often share those struggles and ask them to pray for me.

Instead of making me seem weaker, these admissions made me stronger.

BE CONSISTENT.

Yes, we can do this even when they're away from home. As our Heavenly Father, God is always the same, yesterday, today, and tomorrow. We can help cement that concept in our children's lives when we, as parents, are also consistent.

It's not just important to be consistent with consequences, but also with the good things. From regular family gatherings, to family prayer time, to our own personal devotion time, the kids in our lives are watching us. They know what's important by how regularly we do it.

When they're away from home, this means regular contact through phone calls, video chats, letters, packages, etc. Now is when we have to be careful to keep the lines of communication open. It's easy to let life interfere—for our kids and for us. But that's no excuse. Show them you care by staying in close—consistent—contact.

CATCH THEM IN THE ACT OF BEING GOOD.

Even though you may be separated, don't forget to emphasize the positive. As parents, we can get in a rut of looking for the things our kids do wrong. What we need to do is develop the habit of looking for things they do right.

Studies have shown that the negatives we hear weigh more heavily on us than the positives. To counteract that, we all need more positive reinforcement in our lives. As parents, we have a unique opportunity to build up our children by praising the things they do right, and the things they do well. Don't let distance rob you of this ability.

Even more than building their own self-esteem, this will help them develop the same way of looking for good in others.

Chapter Two

Making Good Choices

The choices our kids make have consequences that reach far beyond what they often realized. We do our best to shepherd and equip them, but ultimately their choices become their own.

Help My Child Do Well in School

Action springs not from thought,
but from a readiness for responsibility.

DIETRICH BONHOEFFER

Dear Lord, I loved the times when I could help my child with homework. Those evenings were about more than just academic success. I got to be a part of his life, helping him decide the best path in the situations he faced. Now he's doing this without me.

I'm praying that You would help him continue to do well in school. Not just the grades he gets, but in all aspects. Remind him of the foundation of faith he comes from.

Put a drive in him to excel. Help him see into the future and the importance of the choices he's making today. Give him insight into which classes to choose when he's planning.

Help him learn to get along with the different instructors and teachers he has. Don't let him be put into a class where he'll be put down or demeaned. Guard his heart as he learns how to deal with different personality types.

As he chooses friends, show him how to find others with the same desire to succeed. Make him a leader in his peer group. Bring out his skills as a peacemaker and encourager. Most of all, let him feel Your presence as You walk beside him every day. Amen.

> *Rather, he must be hospitable, one who loves what is good, who is self-controlled, upright, holy and disciplined.*
>
> TITUS 1:8 NIV

Help My Child Make Wise Choices

The man or woman who is wholly or joyously
surrendered to Christ can't make a wrong choice—
any choice will be the right one.

A. W. TOZER

Dear Lord, when my child is in a new and exciting situation, please don't let her get caught up and carried away when temptation comes. She is away with her friends, and I know it's going to be hard not to go along with the crowd. Let her quickly feel the Spirit's whisper.

Remind her of the foundation You've given her. Make her conscience sharp and active when it comes to the decisions she faces. Keep her from choosing things that will have negative consequences. Especially protect her from things that will affect the rest of her life.

Help her companions reinforce good choices. Let the peer pressure she encounters be a strong, positive influence, not a temptation to stray away from Your path. I know she has a good sense of right and wrong. Don't let that become diluted by her new circumstances.

I know that no one is perfect, and I don't expect that from her. There will be times when she chooses wrong. Give her the courage to admit her mistakes and turn back to You. Don't ever let fear of her past mistakes keep her from coming to You. Amen.

*A fool's way is right in his
own eyes, but whoever listens
to counsel is wise.*
PROVERBS 12:15 HCSB

Help My Child Grow in Wisdom

Patience is the companion of wisdom.

AUGUSTINE

Dear Lord, my child has a lot of new and exciting opportunities right now. Many of them occur when he's away from home, and he has to evaluate them by himself. Give him the strength to know the difference between what's good and what's best. Most of all, give him the strength to say no to the things that he shouldn't pursue.

Growing up is hard. Growing in wisdom is even harder, but that's the heart of what I'm asking for my child. Teach him, through experience, what it means to be wise. Show him how to choose people to help guide his choices.

When people come into his life, give him an internal alarm that goes off if they mean him harm. Help him develop the discernment that will carry him through a lifetime of decision-making.

Show him that wisdom isn't just useful to help us avoid our struggles, but also for getting through a struggle. Remind him that applying wisdom late in a situation is always better than not applying it at all. Amen.

Now if any of you lacks wisdom, he should ask God, who gives to all generously and without criticizing, and it will be given to him.

JAMES 1:5 HCSB

Don't Let My Child Get Away with Wrongdoing

God loves us too much to indulge our every whim.

MAX LUCADO

Dear Lord, sometimes I hesitate when I start to pray for my child. I want his life to be filled with joy and all things that are good. But I also want him to learn the hard lessons that will keep him close to You.

He's far from me, and I don't know what he's doing. I'm praying that he's following the foundation he grew up with. But if he's strayed—even a little—do what it takes to pull him back into line with Your standards in the Bible.

I know it's normal for him to want to spread his wings. Even more than that, I want him to have experiences that solidify his faith and help him move from following our beliefs to making them his own. On the way, though, don't let him stray too far.

Guard him and protect him. Don't let him get away with things that are wrong. Give him a healthy respect for consequences when he makes poor choices. Show him the long-term effects of the choices he's making right now.

Don't let him go through life thinking it's okay to do what you want as long as you don't get caught. Make him into a man of courage who's willing to admit his mistakes and make amends. Amen.

The LORD's eyes see everything; he watches both evil and good people.

PROVERBS 15:3 NCV

Give My Child Wisdom about His Actions

Worry is the cross which we make
for ourselves by overanxiety.

FRANCOIS FENELON

Dear Lord, my child is such a daredevil. I love that he's not afraid to try new things, but I wish he'd temper that fearlessness with some wisdom. I am afraid that if he doesn't learn to think things through, he is going to get hurt.

It was bad enough when he was a toddler and within my sight, but now that he's away from home more, I can't always act as his voice of reason. Please give him just enough consequences so he takes time to think before he acts. He's headstrong and thinks nothing could ever happen to him.

Surround him with friends who are wise. Keep them from rushing into situations that could lead to serious consequences. His choices could affect him in more ways than just physically. Help him develop wisdom about all his actions and their far-reaching effects.

Provide the experiences he needs to temper his decision-making. Guard him from anything that could have negative lifelong results. Help him resist the impulses that will lead him into trouble. Instead, lead him to rely more and more on You. Amen.

*Teach us to number
our days, that we may
gain a heart of wisdom.*
PSALM 90:12 NIV

Thank You for Guiding My Child

The maker of the stars would rather die for you
than live without you. And that is a fact.
So if you need to brag, brag about that.

MAX LUCADO

Dear Lord, I'm watching the decisions my child is making while he's away from home, and I feel so thankful for his choices. I see Your hand of protection and gentle wisdom so clearly in His life.

You have put just the right mix of people in his life. There are those who help him make wise decisions and those who need his help. Continue to give him opportunities to reach out, even as he stays grounded with his faith.

I love getting to watch as he grows and blossoms into an amazing young man. Please use him to share Your love and to be a blessing to others, just as he is to me. Continue to watch over him, surrounding him with friends and companions who have the same desire.

Use him more and more to influence those around him. Give him insight into the different situations he's exposed to. Help him to be an influencer in the lives of others and to always come back to You as his guiding influence. Your love is beyond my imagining, and watching how You love my child leaves me breathless with gratitude. Amen.

As the mountains surround Jerusalem, so the LORD surrounds his people, from this time forth and forevermore.
PSALM 125:2 ESV

Forgive My Parenting Mistakes

Silence, shame, guilt, or any other emotional torment simply
cannot rob us of God's love, of his plan for us.

JO ANN FORE

Dear Lord, I've made so many mistakes as a parent. I've made decisions that have been contrary to Your will, and I know I've hurt my child. Please forgive me. Help me make amends everywhere I can.

I have learned so much about You, Lord, in recent years. Now I realize that some of the things I needed to be a good parent were missing. I have so many regrets about what has gone before, all the things I didn't do right. How do I move past that knowledge? It's hard for me to accept that You forgive me for the things I've done and said. I wish I could go back and do them differently. I know the Bible promises Your forgiveness, and I believe that. Help me to feel that forgiveness, and to forgive myself.

More than that, help me heal any hurts I have inflicted on my child. I know it's not enough to just say a blanket, "I'm sorry." Show me specific instances when I have hurt her, and give me the courage to ask for her forgiveness.

Lord, will You help me to receive Your grace, and for my child to grant me that grace as well. Help us navigate this difficult time with love. Amen.

If we confess our sins, He is faithful and righteous to forgive us our sins and to cleanse us from all unrighteousness.

1 JOHN 1:9 NASB

Help Me to Not Interfere in Your Will

God does not love us because we are valuable.
We are valuable because God loves us.

FULTON SHEEN

Dear Lord, I know that You're teaching my child some valuable lessons right now while she's away from home. My first instinct is to jump in and add my thoughts. Help me to wait on Your promptings before I offer to help. I want to have a positive impact on her life, and I need to know how to do that.

It's so hard to sit back and let her make her own mistakes. I want to protect her, but I know the best protection she'll ever have is to grow closer to You. She won't do that if I'm always inserting myself into her decisions.

This is a new chapter in my life as a parent, and it's more difficult than I thought it would be. There's so much more to raising a child than I ever imagined. I still want to be involved in her life, but I also want to show her that I respect her ability to make good decisions. Help me navigate this new path. Show me how to continue to help her grow without infringing on what You're teaching her.

"But the Advocate, the Holy Spirit, whom the Father will send in my name, will teach you all things and will remind you of everything I have said to you."

JOHN 14:26 NIV

My deepest hope is that she'll always turn to You first, no matter what is going on in her life. Show me how to help that happen, instead of standing in the way. Amen.

Help Me Set Wise Boundaries for My Child

God's work done God's way will never lack God's supply.

HUDSON TAYLOR

Dear Lord, my child is growing up and I'm having to set some new boundaries. He's gone from home more and more. I want to give him the freedom he needs to make good decisions, but I don't want to cut him loose and allow him to be drawn into danger.

This is a time of transition for both of us. I don't want to push him out of the nest, but I also don't want to smother him. Truthfully, I wish for the days when he was safe at home all day long. I worry so much about the things he could run into when he's away.

Give me Your wisdom, Lord. Only You know what lies in his path. You are his true defense, but I want to be used by You to help when I feel the nudge. Help me tell the difference between my desire to help and Your call to intervene.

Show me how to set up wise boundaries. Don't let him resent the fact that he still has rules to follow. He feels like he's all grown up, but he's not quite there yet. Lead me to reasonable consequences when he tests those boundaries and steps over the line.

Don't let any of this damage our relationship or drive him away. Give him insight, too, so he knows this isn't easy for us either. Most of all, help each of us have forgiving hearts when mistakes are made. Amen.

A wise man is cautious and turns away from evil, but a fool is arrogant and careless.

PROVERBS 14:16 NASB

Give Me Confidence in My Parenting Decisions

*Trying to do the Lord's work in your own strength
is the most confusing, exhausting, and tedious of all work.
But when you are filled with the Holy Spirit,
then the ministry of Jesus just flows out of you.*
CORRIE TEN BOOM

Dear Lord, I'm having trouble being confident in my parenting skills and decisions.

Remind me how Your will can still prevail, even when I mess up. I know my focus is once again on what I'm able to do. Help me learn how to rely on You and then have confidence that I'm hearing You correctly.

Parenting is such a dangerous job. It seems that any wrong choice could affect my child for the rest of her life. How could You trust me with such a precious life? I know it's because I'm not really the one who has charge of her life.

You have proven Yourself more than able to take my mistakes and use them to mold her into the woman You want her to be. I've also watched You step in and protect us both when the consequences should have been catastrophic. Thank You for Your faithfulness.

Continue to shore up my confidence in You. Make sure I walk closely with You, so that all my parenting decisions come from You. Amen.

For the LORD will be your confidence and will keep your foot from being caught.
PROVERBS 3:26 NASB

Don't Forget to Feed Yourself

Right now you have plenty and can help those who are in need.
Later, they will have plenty and can share with you
when you need it. In this way, things will be equal.

2 CORINTHIANS 8:14 NLT

As a full-time writer and speaker, I spend a good deal of time on airplanes. So much, that I tend to ignore the flight attendant's spiel at the beginning of the ride, instructing passengers what to do in case of an emergency. So I was taken aback when the lady sitting beside me commented on what she heard. "That makes no sense at all."

I looked up to see what set her off and saw the oxygen mask dangling from the stewardess's hand.

She continued commenting on the instructions. "If I was traveling with a child or someone who needed help, I'd put their mask on first."

I smiled again and returned to the papers I'd brought to work on, unwilling to be drawn into conversation. It was the last leg of my journey, and all I wanted was to get home to my husband and sons. But I couldn't quit thinking about the instructions and possible scenarios. At first, my seatmate's opinion seemed unselfish and even vaguely Christlike. But the longer I considered the implications, the more I began to disagree with her viewpoint. The flight attendant's instructions were rooted in truth—spiritual truth about parenting.

It is not possible to share something I don't possess.

How could I equip my growing children to inhale the breath

41

of God if I had no breath myself? The thought made me think about how my priorities had drifted. Our lives were insanely busy, and I'd been using that—and feelings of guilt about the selfishness of spending time on me—let my own regular quiet time with God slip to the wayside.

My kids are just as busy as I am—with schoolwork, activities, and friends—and they're away from home more and more. Instead of equipping them to manage their time wisely, I was showing them that it was okay to let busyness overshadow the importance of time with God.

That jolt of truth helped me to readjust my life back into alignment. I saw clearly that time alone with God wasn't selfish, it was foundational. I had to let Him fill me up before I could be of any good to anyone else—and it was a lesson I decided I'd model for my kids.

Learn How to Pray

The effective prayer of a righteous man can accomplish much.
Elijah was a man with a nature like ours, and he prayed
earnestly that it would not rain, and it did not rain on the
earth for three years and six months. Then he prayed again,
and the sky poured rain and the earth produced its fruit.

JAMES 5:16–18 NASB

Many people are surprised to learn that prayer didn't come naturally to me. That seems odd considering I write entire books of prayers. But I had a lot of preconceived ideas that I had to move past before I could gain any traction with my prayer life.

One of the biggest obstacles I faced was that I truly believed if I loved God, and if I loved my children then the prayers would just flow. I thought the words would pour out of me in beautiful lines of powerful entreaty.

That wasn't what came out.

My prayers were pitiful, messy requests. The words were not beautifully orchestrated; instead they were often incoherent and punctuated with tears. Beyond that, prayer was hard work. It wasn't something that just happened out of the overflow. I had to work at it.

Underlying all my frustration was the secret fear that somehow my prayers weren't good enough. I felt like there was some sort of holiness quotient that I was falling short of. That terrified me. As my kids continued to grow, I knew prayer was the lifeline I needed to be an active part of keeping them safe.

Even knowing that, my frustration kept me from a consistent practice of prayer.

Then, in my quiet time one morning, I reread these verses in James. Initially they seemed to reinforce all my fears. What I saw was only that to have an effective prayer life, I'd have to be like the biblical giants of old.

But when I dug deeper, God brought something to mind I'd never considered. I remembered that early on in Israel's history, God had warned them that if they didn't obey Him, He'd withhold blessings, specifically the blessing of rain. I felt hope begin to blossom. I immediately turned to Deuteronomy 11 and there it was—God's warning that He would shut up the heavens if they turned from Him.

My heart leapt. Righteous prayer wasn't based on my ability to say the right words. It was based on God's righteousness.

Elijah's prayer was effective because he knew God, and he prayed God's own words back to Him. God would always be true to His Word. I felt a floodgate of possibilities open up. I didn't need to come up with the right words; God had already given them to me.

That was all the encouragement I needed. Now when I was at a loss for words about how to pray for my kids, I only had to open my Bible and use God's words.

So Who's Really Driving the Car?

> *Teach me to do your will, for you are my God;*
> *may your good Spirit lead me on level ground.*
> PSALM 143:10 NIV

There are times in my life when making the right decision seems like a no-brainer. Unfortunately those times are few and far between.

I tend to be a little bit of a control freak. That character trait often makes it difficult to follow God unconditionally. Let me give you an example.

When our oldest child was just a few months old, my husband and I felt like God was calling us to leave our home in Arkansas, and move to South Carolina. We had no friends or family in the Carolinas, but my husband had a job offer, and there had been some issues with his job in Arkansas that made both of us uncomfortable. So we began to discuss the possibilities. My husband, ever the engineer, made lists of pros and cons. While I, the creative right-brained one, tried to discover how I *felt* about the chance of moving. We wrangled over the decision for weeks, but for every pro there was a con, and for every upside there was a corresponding downside. The situation had us stymied.

Then one night, as I drifted off, I was captivated by a dream. I was the passenger in a car, a convertible to be exact, and we were driving a dangerous, winding road that led up the side of a mountain. The road was a tiny, two-lane affair, minus guardrails. There were granite cliffs on the mountain side of the road, and a sheer drop to the valley below on the other. I knew about the drop-off because the driver kept veering toward the edge of the cliff and

I'd have to reach over and yank the steering wheel to keep us from crashing into the valley below. As we hurtled toward the top of the mountain, we were up so high I could occasionally see clouds below us.

Finally, I got really irritated because it seemed the higher we got, the more often I'd have to pull us back from the edge, and it suddenly occurred to me I didn't know who was driving. While I kept a cautionary hand on the steering wheel, I risked a quick glance at the face of the person driving. Even though I couldn't describe the features to you now, I immediately recognized Him . . . it was Jesus driving the car.

I was mortified, and I jerked my hand away from the wheel and sure enough, He drove us right off the edge of the mountain. But we didn't crash. No, instead we were suddenly free, and soaring above the mountain. I don't remember Him saying anything, but He held tightly to my hand, and I remember Him smiling.

At this point I woke, and I shook my husband awake to tell him about my dream. He got excited and gave me a hug, "That's it. That's the answer."

I was still a little groggy, and I voiced the first thought that came to me. "Okay, but what's the question?"

He laughed and hugged me again. "That's our answer about moving. We've been trying to make the decision all by ourselves. God wants us to just let go and follow Him."

Within the month we were gone, headed to South Carolina. It has been one of the single-best decisions we've ever made. That decision caused a domino effect in our lives leading us straight to God and equipping us to grow in faith as we trusted Him with our children. Learning to let go of control—especially as our kids are more and more away from home—has strengthened our faith and our family.

Is It Failure or Actually Fruit in Disguise?

> But the fruit of the Spirit is love, joy, peace, patience,
> kindness, goodness, faithfulness, gentleness, self-control;
> against such things there is no law.
>
> GALATIANS 5:22–23 NASB

I spent a lot of time with other parents while my kids were growing up. We'd gather at church, PTA meetings, sometimes just in line at the grocery store. But wherever we congregated, there was one thing I could count on. We'd begin to compare notes on parenting.

As we compared the routes we'd traveled in parenting, I noticed many similarities to my own. Most were like mine—not a direct route—but a circuitous trip full of bumps and detours. Frequently a parent's path is littered with broken dreams and shattered expectations.

At the time, I thought of them as failures.

But looking back, I can see them as something else. Those instances in my kids' lives that I'd always labeled as my failures and shortcomings had changed. Now, in the light of the amazing men they'd become, I saw those detours differently. They hadn't been failures, they'd really been opportunities for my kids to grow and learn.

Those times of waiting had become patience.

The weeks—and sometimes months—of frustration had become discipline.

The heartbreaking rejections became joy as God's plan began to emerge in their young lives.

All those difficult circumstances I'd tried to protect them from had been used by God to teach them things they needed to know. They'd had to experience the failures to get strong, as well as develop compassion for others on similar journeys. He'd even used my failures as a parent to their benefit.

Somewhere along the way, God used the seeds of failure and frustration to grow fruit in their lives and mine. I challenge you to look at those things you've labeled failure, and notice the fruit that's now begun to grow.

Am I Causing
an Unscheduled Stop?

> *So Miriam was shut up outside the camp for seven days,*
> *and the people did not move on until Miriam was received again.*
> NUMBERS 12:15 NASB

Miriam's sin brought the entire nation of Israel to a screeching halt for seven days while God dealt with her and brought her back in line with His will. It must have been devastating for Miriam to realize she was the cause of an unscheduled stop.

How do I know? Because I've discovered that any of us can become Miriam and bring a family skidding to a stop.

This particular time, I was playing the role of Miriam.

Have you ever said yes to something because you thought you should, or continued serving even though God was leading you in a different direction? In my zeal to serve God, I've once again run ahead of His will and put myself in the position of control. I'd traveled far from God and our entire family was paying the price.

My kids were growing up, and spending more and more time out of my sight. I fretted and worried about all the what-ifs that crossed my mind. I was convinced that it was part of my job to anticipate all the things that could go wrong and have contingency plans in place—just in case.

I weighed my sons down with warnings, illustrating them with stories of what had happened in other families.

My worry was driving my sons—and my husband—crazy.

While reading this passage one morning, I had my wake-up call from God. Somewhere along the way, I'd decided that their well-being rested on my abilities instead of God's. This misalignment added to my fears about what was happening when they were out of my sight.

This realization wasn't easy to swallow. I felt like I was doing something when I worried. But I swallowed my fear—and my pride—and I confessed what I'd done to God and handed Him back the reins of control for my kids.

As I once again aligned myself with God's will and let Him be the only one in charge, the tension began to recede as God's peace once again flooded the house. As I relearned the lesson of listening, the stress receded and the joy of parenting returned.

GIVE YOUR KIDS ROOM TO FAIL.

In some ways this seems like the opposite of making good choices, but what it does is help them develop the skill to make good choices. This is particularly important when they're away from us, and it's even harder to do then.

Watching our kids choose something we know isn't going to turn out well can be heartbreaking. By doing so, though, we help them stretch and grow as they learn that failure isn't always as bad as they think. We never want to gloat over unwise choices or use the phrase, "I told you so."

We want to model the behavior of God. When we've chosen wrongly, He's there to comfort us, forgive us, and help us get back on the right track. We want to be that kind of parent to our kids.

YOU CAN'T SHARE WHAT YOU HAVEN'T LEARNED, AND YOU CAN'T GET WATER OUT OF AN EMPTY WELL.

Ouch. This is one I've struggled with over the years. It means that I have to keep learning about God and nurturing my relationship with Him. I've especially needed deep reservoirs to help me when my kids were away from home.

Spending regular time with God gives me the ability to be a better parent. When I let God fill me up, I have a full foundation of patience, love, and forgiveness. When I'm running on empty, I often have none of those things to give to my kids.

BE YOUR CHILD'S ADVOCATE.

There are times when your child will be wrongly accused. We must be willing to believe in them and defend them—especially from a distance. Sometimes that means listening and encouraging their choices. Sometimes it means traveling to where they are to help make things right.

This doesn't mean we shield them from reasonable consequences when they are wrong, but we're there to support them no matter what they've gotten themselves into. God would never abandon us, and we must make that decision in regard to our own children.

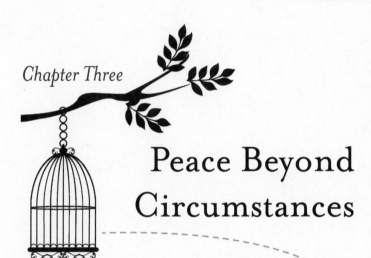

Chapter Three

Peace Beyond Circumstances

There are times in our lives—and the lives of our children—when life gets turned upside down. We may be facing a catastrophe or just a time of stress. Regardless, that's when it's most important to look beyond the situation to find the peace we so desperately crave.

Cover My Child with Peace

Rest and be thankful.
WILLIAM WORDSWORTH

Dear Lord, I'm asking You to watch over my child tonight while he's away from home. It is hard to be young and away from what's familiar, even if it's exciting. Remind him that You're right there with him.

I'm asking You to speak to him clearly. Give him the confirmation he needs right now. Show him the doors You're opening for him. I know that You have plans for him and that You love him in ways we can't imagine.

Help him to feel Your presence. Cover him with peace. Let him see some of the purposes for what he's been through. Surround him with people who will confirm what You have for him.

Give him the comfort he needs right now and protect him from fear, anxiety, or despair. You are a God of answers, and I thank You for never giving up on any of us. Amen.

God is our refuge and strength, a very present help in trouble.
PSALM 46:1 NASB

Grant My Child Peace
When Overcome with Fear

I'm not afraid of storms, for I'm learning how to sail my ship.

LOUISA MAY ALCOTT

Dear Lord, I ache for my child. Life can be so scary at times. I imagine she feels like she is all alone sometimes.

I know You are a refuge of peace within the storms of life. I pray that she will experience that truth right now. Wrap Your arms around her and hold her close. Allow her to physically feel You standing between her and chaos. Remind her that You will never leave her or forsake her.

The Bible tells us we shouldn't live in fear, but sometimes that is very hard to do. Bring to mind instances where You have triumphed over incredible odds. Let her see Your might at work defending her and all those she holds dear. Most of all, don't let her feel alone. As she feels Your presence, also send her friends to stand with her through this tumultuous time. Amen.

The LORD is my light and my salvation—whom should I fear? The LORD is the stronghold of my life—of whom should I be afraid?

PSALM 27:1 HCSB

Give My Child Hope for the Future

He that lives in hope dances without music.

GEORGE HERBERT

Dear Lord, I'm asking You to give my child big dreams. I want him to reach for the stars and become the person You have intended for him to be. Don't let anything that happens in his life now destroy his hope.

It's easy to get caught up in the things we can't do, but I want him to look at the future as a place of infinite possibilities. Keep him from making the mistakes that I did. I know I've put arbitrary limits on what I think is possible.

Remind him that Your path doesn't hinge on his perfection. You work as well in our weaknesses and failures as in our strengths and successes. Draw him closer to You and open his mind to all that he can do.

You created him with hopes, so help him learn that the mistakes of today don't destroy the dreams of tomorrow. Lord, You are faithful even when we are faithless. Make that concept real in his life right now. Amen.

> *Now the One who provides seed for the sower and bread for food will provide and multiply your seed and increase the harvest of your righteousness.*
>
> 2 CORINTHIANS 9:10 HCSB

Surround My Child with Peace

Worry is a cycle of inefficient thoughts
whirling around a center of fear.

CORRIE TEN BOOM

Dear Lord, even though my child is young, I'm noticing a disturbing tendency. She's worried about everything. I don't want her childhood to be filled with stress. I want it to be filled with joy.

When she feels bad physically, keep fearful thoughts from her mind. Reassure her that there are adults in her life who love her and will take care of her. Remind her that there are people who love her and are watching over her.

Don't let her get weighed down with anxiety and feel even worse physically. Surround her with friends who will have a positive outlook. Give her new, exciting experiences that take her mind off of things to worry about.

Renew her courage to try new things and not worry about getting hurt. I don't want her to become reckless, but I'm praying for a sense of adventure to fill her once again. Most of all, show her that You are always there for her. Amen.

"I have told you these things, so that in me you may have peace. In this world you will have trouble. But take heart! I have overcome the world."

JOHN 16:33 NIV

Take Away My Child's Loneliness

God cannot give us a happiness and peace
apart from Himself, because it is not there.
There is no such thing.

C. S. LEWIS

Dear Lord, please help my child when she is lonely. She's in a new place and struggling to get comfortable with her new life. It's an exciting time, but she's left behind friends whom she's come to rely on. Don't let her be overwhelmed by loneliness.

Help her reach out to others around her and make new friends. Bring new friends into her life who have the same struggles. Give them opportunities to encourage each other and help one another through difficult times. Show her how to balance new friends with old ones. Most of all, keep her faith solid.

Don't let her give in to the loneliness and retreat. Help her have the courage to venture out and try new things. Connect her with companions who share her interests. Surround her with friends who know You and can help her stay strong. Amen.

*All my longings lie open
before you, Lord; my sighing
is not hidden from you.*

PSALM 38:9 NIV

Help My Child Overcome Her Shyness

Doubts and mistrust are the mere panic of
timid imagination, which the steadfast heart will conquer,
and the large mind transcend.

HELEN KELLER

Dear Lord, be with my child when she feels shy. Now that she's away from home more, I worry that her fears will become overwhelming. Use this time to take away this struggle.

Give her insight into her feelings. Help her find creative ways to move past this.

Don't let her focus in on herself, her faults, and her limits. Take away those negative thoughts and replace them with a clear image of how You view her. Lend her Your eyes to see the truth about herself, her strengths, and her value.

There is so much about my child that's precious. Her gift of encouragement is such a strength. Put friends in her life to help her focus on what she has to offer instead of what she's lacking.

Don't let her insecurities keep her from stepping out and following the path You have for her. Replace her shyness with boldness. Most of all, whisper confidence into her ear, and help her to feel Your comforting presence when she is fearful. Amen.

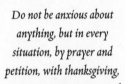

Do not be anxious about anything, but in every situation, by prayer and petition, with thanksgiving, present your requests to God. And the peace of God, which transcends all understanding, will guard your hearts and your minds in Christ Jesus.

PHILIPPIANS 4:6–7 NIV

Help Me, I'm Scared

God incarnate is the end of fear; and the heart that
realizes that He is in the midst . . .
will be quiet in the middle of alarm.

F.B. MEYER

Dear Lord, I'm scared; my child is away from home for the first time. I don't know exactly where she is or what she's doing. I thought this time would be exciting. Instead, for me, it's terrifying. We talk on the phone, but I struggle with not knowing what she is doing all the time. The possibility of those secrets worry me. Help me sort out fear from truth.

I have the perspective of years, and I know that some of the decisions she's making now will have long-reaching consequences. She sees the fun going on around her and just wants to join in. She's searching for new experiences. I want her to grow, but I want that growth to be safe and protected.

Give me Your peace as I learn to be a parent during this new season. Help my child trust me and confide what's going on in her life. When we disagree, make sure I do so in love. Don't let my worries and my words drive her further from me.

Surround her with new friends who share her values. As they go out, help them encourage each other to stay true to what they know is right. Don't let peer pressure affect them negatively.

Pull her in close to You. Don't let her forget Your love for her. Amen.

*"Have I not commanded you?
Be strong and courageous.
Do not be afraid; do not be
discouraged, for the LORD
your God will be with you
wherever you go."*

JOSHUA 1:9 NIV

Calm My Anxious Thoughts

I do not want merely to possess a faith,
I want a faith that possesses me.

CHARLES KINGSLEY

Dear Lord, my child is away from home and I'm worried about everything that could happen. My thoughts are my enemies as I imagine all the horrible possibilities. I know that You are trustworthy in everything, but it's so hard for me to let go of the worry when it comes to her. Help me. Please calm my anxious thoughts.

I thought I was stronger than this. But when it comes to my child, I'm not. I know only too well that the world is a dangerous place. I'm not there with my child to protect her, and it scares me. I have to remember that the responsibility of her safety ultimately lies with You. Remind me of all the ways You've taken care of her before. Bring to mind Bible verses that speak of Your faithfulness.

In spite of how fearful I feel, use this situation to grow my faith. Make me stronger and more certain of who You are and how much You love us. I don't want to be afraid, but I'm struggling right now. Put people in my life to help shore up my courage. Forgive me for my lack of faith, and help me rest in You as You take care of her. Amen.

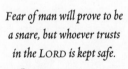

Fear of man will prove to be a snare, but whoever trusts in the LORD is kept safe.

PROVERBS 29:25 NIV

Help Me Love a Parent Who Receives Bad News

First keep peace with yourself,
then you can also bring peace to others.
THOMAS À KEMPIS

Dear Lord, my heart is breaking for my friend. She's received bad news about her child, and I don't know how to reach out to her. I want to be there for her, but I don't want the fact that my child is safe to add to her pain. Show me how to be the friend she needs.

I'm battling between relief and fear. My child is also away from home, and I'm so grateful he's safe. But if something tragic can happen to someone I know, it seems all the more likely it can happen to us. Please keep my child safe from all harm.

Don't let me be self-focused right now. Show me how to reach out to this hurting family. My fear could keep me from getting involved. I don't want to know how similar our circumstances could be. Lord, pull me out of myself and use me to show Your love to my friends.

Use this to remind me that You are in control and that even if something bad happens, You're still there. I don't want to believe this can occur, but we live in a scary world. Remind me how Your faithfulness goes beyond circumstances and You are always with us. Amen.

A friend loves at all times, and a brother is born for a time of adversity.
PROVERBS 17:17 NIV

Restore Our Relationship

We win by tenderness. We conquer by forgiveness.
FREDERICK W. ROBERTSON

Dear Lord, I've let arguments and disagreements come between my child and me. She's away from home more and more, and these hurts are affecting us. Show me how to repair our relationship. Show me the difference between childish resentment from her at reasonable discipline and what I need to ask forgiveness for. I want to be a good parent—loving and consistent—but it's so hard.

Help me reach through her anger with love and repair our relationship. I know that there have been times when I've lashed out in ways that hurt her. Now I'm ready to admit I've let my feelings of shame drive us even further apart.

It's time to stop blaming and work on healing. I'm praying that I'm not too late. Show me how to begin the process.

Take away any hurts I feel from the things she's done, even if she never acknowledges them. Give me the courage to own up to my mistakes and accept responsibility for all I've said and done. I want her to know how much I love her and want to be an active part of her life. I'm scared she won't accept that.

Go before me and smooth a path to reconciliation between us. Soften her heart toward me and let her see my intentions and my love. Restore our broken relationship and bring us closer to You in the process. Amen.

> *He who conceals a transgression seeks love, but he who repeats a matter separates intimate friends.*
> PROVERBS 17:9 NASB

The Problem with Independence

> *Take pains with these things; be absorbed in them,*
> *so that your progress will be evident to all.*
>
> 1 TIMOTHY 4:15 NASB

We spend all our childrens' lives teaching them to be independent. Then, when they up and do something to express their independence, it's painful. Parenting is an exercise in contradictions. I first ran into the pain of independence early. Our boys were just toddlers when they started standing on their own.

I remember one particular Sunday. We were taking number-two child to the nursery at a new church. As we approached we could hear the howls from terrified two- and three-year-olds unhappy about being separated from their parents. Our child squirmed to get out of my husband's arms. As he put him down, his daddy and I exchanged glances, half-expecting him to bolt in the other direction. Instead, he led the way toward the chaos.

We waited our turn to get name badges and pass our child over the half-door to the workers. Things went without a hitch. Our towheaded toddler went to the worker with a grin and immediately joined a group of happy kids exploring the toy bins. Other parents shot us frustrated glances, and I was torn between pride and grief. The arrow in my heart seemed to say that he no longer needed or cared about us.

My husband was gleeful. He grabbed my hand and smiled down at me. "That went well."

I couldn't answer, and tears welled up in my eyes. He frowned and looked down at me. "What's wrong?"

"He doesn't need me." The words were forced past the lump in my throat.

My husband pulled me into his arms. "Of course he needs you. This just means we've given him the confidence he needs to feel comfortable in new situations. We should be celebrating a job well done, not mourning because he's not screaming in the nursery."

He was right, of course. I couldn't help but draw a parallel with God and His children. He wants us to need Him. But He also expects us to grow, learning how to stand and be strong.

Learning to Laugh Through the Hard Stuff

> *Your ears shall hear a word behind you, saying,*
> *"This is the way, walk in it," whenever you turn*
> *to the right hand or whenever you turn to the left.*
>
> ISAIAH 30:21 NKJV

There's a fine line we all have to walk as parents. We want to sympathize with and comfort our kids, but we also want to equip them to walk through the hard knocks of life instead of collapsing and expecting the world to stop when they are bumped and bruised.

I began to find my own balance with this when the boys were young. Like any toddlers, our kids were prone to tumbles. Instead of rushing to them and making a big deal about their minor falls, I would clap my hands and giggle, encouraging them to keep going and not give in to tears. Early on, their response was confusion. Their little chins would wobble as they tried to decide if Mommy was playing a bad joke on them. But invariably, they couldn't resist the fun and began smiling and clapping as well.

Truthfully, I think it went deeper than just the distraction of fun. Our boys changed the way they looked at the tumbles of life because they trusted us. Of course we'd rush to help them when something more serious happened. They knew we wouldn't make light of something that was a serious injury. But we endeavored to teach them that the little falls, while they might sting for a moment, were just that—little. My boys now know how to pick themselves up, brush themselves off, and keep going.

God is the same way. He doesn't want us to dwell on the daily struggles of life, but He cares deeply about *all* the things we care about. He's a Father we can depend on, but He doesn't want the little things to keep us from going after the big things. We can trust Him to guide us as we navigate the obstacles in our paths.

Turning Please to Thanksgiving

*I know what it is to be in need, and I know what it is
to have plenty. I have learned the secret of being content
in any and every situation, whether well fed or hungry,
whether living in plenty or in want.*

PHILIPPIANS 4:12 NIV

We live in a material world. Everywhere we turn, someone is trying to sell us on the idea that things and circumstances lead to happiness. If I just have the perfect house, car, kids, husband, wife, etc., then I'll be content. The list keeps getting longer. If something gets crossed off, three more things take its place. Raising kids who aren't focused on having and getting is tough.

This laundry list of things we desire even invaded our prayer time with our kids. This list isn't full of bad things. Often they're a request for them—or others—to get well, be protected, or get something they desire. But no matter how good the things on the list are, they miss the point. Our focus wasn't in the right place.

When this realization hit me, I began trying to change the focus of my prayer life. I made a purposeful decision to move from a list of *please*, to a list of *thanksgiving*. Because truthfully, if we spent every second of every day that we have left thanking God for the way He's blessed us, we couldn't cover it all.

We didn't give up praying for others. But we threw away the laundry list. In addition to prayers for healing and salvation, we added the request for contentment beside the name of everyone we prayed for.

As my boys grow and leave home, I want them to understand and experience what Paul described. I want them to know the depth of contentment he wrote about, no matter what circumstances surrounded them. I want us all to be so confident in God's provision that we can face anything with peace and thanksgiving.

Solid Ground

{ *And You have not given me over into the hand of the enemy;*
You have set my feet in a large place.
PSALM 31:8 NASB }

My husband and I love living here in the foothills of the Blue Ridge Mountains. We enjoy hiking and camping and all manner of outdoor activities. While the boys were young, we always tried to set aside at least one weekend a year for the two of us to slip away. Frequently that getaway took place in the mountains.

One year, we decided to take that time and camp in the Smoky Mountains. We spent that Saturday hiking. We had decided to try out a trail that was a little more strenuous than what we normally chose. It was a gorgeous morning when we started out, and, although the trail was steep, it wasn't unmanageable.

We continued along the trail, but it became so steep that I began to wonder how the view from the top of any mountain could be worth this type of climb. As we neared the summit, the trail was so precarious ropes had been added to the rock face to give hikers a place to hold on to. Not my idea of a relaxing way to spend time, but we were already committed so we decided to push on.

Finally, we let go of the last rope and scrambled the last few feet to the top of the mountain. We were standing on flat, solid ground with an amazing vista laid out before us. We could see part of the trail below and the mountain we'd just climbed. Also, as far as the eye could see, lay the gray-blue outlines of the mountains. They were highlighted with intense bursts of red and orange from the fall foliage. It was a sight that took my breath away and had definitely been worth the climb.

So often when we're in the midst of seemingly insurmountable trials, especially as parents, we forget the resources we have in God. But He will always rescue us—and even more importantly our kids—by providing the handholds we need and pulling us up. Then He sets us firmly on solid ground, with a new perspective of all that's passed before.

For me, some of the toughest parenting times were the result of something that had happened when I wasn't with my child. But this visual stays with me. I know that God will give me the perspective I need to face any challenge as long as I hold tightly to Him.

Fearing the Right Things

The fear of the LORD is a fountain of life,
turning people away from the snares of death.
PROVERBS 14:27 HCSB

As parents, we easily let fear overwhelm us. Every decision we make seems to carry the certainty of calamity. We let the possibility of disaster stand between us and the peace of God. We worry about hurting our kids, hurting others; even the opinions of others bring with them terror-inducing consequences.

We all struggle against this deadly enemy. No, I didn't misspeak. Fear is deadly. It strangles all hope, killing our dreams with a dreaded whisper of *what-if*.

But what if fear isn't always a death sentence for our dreams? What if the right kind of fear could propel us into fulfilling our callings?

I'd like to propose that we're afraid of the wrong things.

Instead of fearing that our child won't be popular, what if we feared that they wouldn't reach out to others who are different? Instead of fearing that they'll be ridiculed or made fun of, what if we feared they wouldn't take a stand for something that matters? Instead of fearing they'll somehow fall short of success, what if we feared they wouldn't make an effort at all?

I've had to make a decision to turn around and redirect the fear I feel in the right direction. How about you? What fear do you need to redirect to once again get back in the middle of the path God has for you and for your kids?

PICK YOUR BATTLES.

Parenting is a process of letting go, and that's never more true than when our kids are far away. We are teaching our kids to stand on their own, and that brings with it a myriad of possible battles. Everyone makes it to adulthood by a different path, and while we may not always agree on the path, it's the journey that's important.

We can fill our relationships with unwelcome strife if we fight our kids on every issue. We have to pick and choose what's most important and go to the mat on those issues. For example, in our lives one issue we chose not to fight about was the length and style of hair our boys chose. While we would have preferred it short and neat, as long as it was clean, we accepted long and shaggy. At the end of the day, we have to cultivate peace in our relationships, even if it means our teenaged boys have long hair.

I DON'T HAVE TO SAY EVERYTHING I THINK.

We live in a sound-bite society. We watch television and movies where every line is designed to get a laugh or make a point. Life can't be like that. We're not on stage, and the people around us aren't actors. Those close to us can be hurt by our words if we're not careful, especially when those words come through a telephone or e-mail. Long-distance conversation takes work.

ENCOURAGE HEALTHY FINANCIAL CHOICES.

When our kids are away from us, it can be tempting to show our love by buying things for them. We want to emphasize other ways to show our love. Some of us also enjoy shopping with our kids. Hearing about the things they're acquiring when they're away from us can be a point of connection. It can also turn from something good to something unhealthy. Help your kids find other ways to find joy beyond the material things they possess.

Chapter Four

True
Self-Confidence

More than anything, we want our kids to be able to face what comes in life. But their confidence and resilience must be set in a bedrock of truth about Whose they are, instead of just who they are.

Help My Child Discover Your Purpose for His Life

All that God requires of us is an opportunity
to show what He can do.

A. B. SIMPSON

Dear Lord, I know that You have a purpose for each of us. Deep inside we long to know and fulfill that purpose. We want to know that our lives have meaning beyond ourselves. I also know that my child isn't too young to begin connecting with that purpose.

Populate his life with people who will give him Your perspective. Surround him with friends who are also striving to find Your path in their lives. Make them traveling companions on this journey toward Your will.

Give him wise mentors and instructors who will speak Your truth. Make them men and women of integrity who have my child's best interests in their heart. As they guide him, give him discernment and the ability to tell the difference between Your truth and the world's lies.

There are those who would not want him to follow You closely. Let him see their motives and be able to stay clear of their influence. Show him how Your path is the most wonderful adventure he could ever imagine. Amen.

"I am the vine, you are the branches; he who abides in Me and I in him, he bears much fruit, for apart from Me you can do nothing."

JOHN 15:5 NASB

Protect My Child from the Influence of Pornography

Love is the great conqueror of lust.

C. S. LEWIS

Dear Lord, I don't want to have to pray about this in regard to my child, but I know pornography is everywhere in our society. I also know that You can protect him. I hate that kids today have ready access to it.

I can't always be there to keep him safe, but You can. Guard him and make it difficult for him to access any inappropriate images that may tempt him. Do whatever it takes to keep him from viewing anything that could harm him now or later in his life. Don't let him share images of pornography with anyone either.

If he has seen things he shouldn't, I'm asking You to remove those images from his mind. I know the images he views now can have a negative effect throughout his life.

Surround him with friends who also have a desire to remain pure. Make sure they have the courage to hold one another accountable. Give them opportunities to share their fears and desires. Prompt them to hold tight to Your standards of right and wrong. Don't let them drift from Your truth when temptations come. Amen.

Flee immorality. Every other sin that a man commits is outside the body, but the immoral man sins against his own body.

1 CORINTHIANS 6:18 NASB

Protect My Child from Becoming Materialistic

Holiness is an unselfing of ourselves.

FREDERICK W. FABER

Dear Lord, my child is struggling with materialism. I can see him putting more and more value on what he does and doesn't have. He knows that we're not supposed to gauge our worth by possessions, but that knowledge doesn't seem to be enough.

I know it is hard when others have some things that he would like to have. We live in a culture where self-worth is tied to what we have. Don't let him begin to use what people buy him as a measure of how much they love him. Help him see past that lie.

Surround him with friends who know that true worth doesn't come from what we own. Let him see the true motives of those who would shower him with gifts to win his love. I wish I could give him all that he wants, but I know that wouldn't be a healthy thing. Still, don't let him resent me for what I can't provide for him.

Give him a healthier perspective about life than just as a race to gather more stuff. Show him how much You love him, and that Your blessings can't be limited by physical possessions. Shower him with Your love and truth. Amen.

Your life should be free from the love of money. Be satisfied with what you have, for He Himself has said, I will never leave you or forsake you.

HEBREWS 13:5 HCSB

Help My Child See Her Beauty

Since love grows within you, so beauty grows.
For love is the beauty of the soul.
AUGUSTINE

Dear Lord, my child is going through a difficult stage. She doesn't have a healthy self-image, and I'm fearful of where that insecurity could lead her.

I've tried to help her develop an accurate sense of beauty and worth. But suddenly all her self-esteem is wrapped up in how she *should* look. She has a skewed view of what a girl her age—and women in general—should look like.

Everywhere she turns, she's bombarded with unrealistic images of how she should look. She knows so many of the pictures she sees are retouched, but she's ignoring that fact. Even her moods are affected by whether or not she lives up to the ideals she has adopted as realistic.

There are so many suffering today because they place too much emphasis on physical beauty. Help her redefine what it means to be beautiful by conforming her ideals to Your standards.

To You, my child is beautiful. You judge the heart, and I'm praying that she can begin to understand what this means. Show her the beauty that she possesses is more than any image. Amen.

I praise you because I am fearfully and wonderfully made; your works are wonderful, I know that full well.
PSALM 139:14 NIV

Help My Child Value Modesty

Character is what a man is in the dark.

D. L. MOODY

Dear Lord, my child is growing up and he's being exposed to so much right now. He's having to decide what is and isn't appropriate behavior between a man and a woman. Give him wisdom as he interacts with the girls in his life.

The examples we're all bombarded with through the media are not standards You have set for us. Everywhere he turns, he's hit with standards that aren't healthy. Men, as well as women, need to conduct themselves in a manner that falls in line with Your Word. Remind him of those standards and help him rely on them as he navigates the minefield of male/female relationships.

Put people in his life who are good examples in this regard. Help him find a group of friends who have the same faith foundation. Show them how to hold one another accountable, in dress, deed, and dating.

Help him make wise choices when he decides what's appropriate to wear. Protect him from temptation when he's with others. Show him the value of modesty, in himself and in the girls he hangs out with. Amen.

How can a young man keep his way pure? By keeping it according to Your word.

PSALM 119:9 NASB

Protect My Child from Perfectionism

Failure is a school in which the truth always grows strong.

HENRY WARD BEECHER

Dear Lord, please keep my child from being obsessed with being perfect; it's leading him places that are dangerous. He's discouraged by his performance in school, sports, even hobbies. I don't know how to counteract this. I need Your help.

His desire to be the best is out of perspective. He wavers between despair and egotism. He's making assumptions about how others view him based on his own distorted view of who he thinks he should be.

As he falls further and further behind in his strive for perfection, I watch him struggle with how he communicates with others about himself. Help him find a healthy way to deal with that.

Please step in and stop this vicious cycle. Readjust his view and bring it back in line with Your truth. Use the people around him to show him that he's loved because of who he is, not how he performs. Give him such a foundation of love and faith in You that his concept of who he should be changes to Your vision. Amen.

> But He said to me, "My grace is sufficient for you, for power is perfected in weakness." Therefore, I will most gladly boast all the more about my weaknesses, so that Christ's power may reside in me.
>
> 2 CORINTHIANS 12:9 HCSB

Give Me Your Perspective

Give to us clear vision that we may know where to stand
and what to stand for—because unless we stand
for something, we shall fall for anything.

PETER MARSHALL

Dear Lord, I hate when my child is away from me. I want her to be out with her friends and enjoy life, but the worries I have about what could happen while she's gone destroy that. I'm trying to be supportive of her as she grows, but it seems like she's leaving me behind. I need Your perspective so I can get through this.

I'm fearful about so many things that can go wrong with her situation. I know the Bible assures me that You bring good out of every situation. But I remember being where she is in life. I made so many mistakes, and I want her to be protected from those life-long consequences.

True, I wouldn't be who I am today without those experiences. But going through them was so horrible. I don't want to watch her struggle like that.

Show me how You're working in her life right now. I know You're there, even when she doesn't acknowledge You. Let me see with Your eyes and grant me the peace I so desperately crave.

More than that, use me to share Your perspective with her. Let me have a place in her life. Make sure she knows how much You and I both love her. Amen.

> *"For my thoughts are not your thoughts, neither are your ways my ways," declares the LORD. "As the heavens are higher than the earth, so are my ways higher than your ways and my thoughts than your thoughts."*
>
> ISAIAH 55:8–9 NIV

I Feel So Powerless

*Do not strive in your own strength; cast yourself at the feet
of the Lord Jesus, and wait upon Him in the sure confidence
that He is with you, and works in you.*

<small>ANDREW MURRAY</small>

Dear Lord, there's so much going on in my child's life right now, and I'm powerless to help. I want to be there with him, giving him the physical help and emotional support he needs. Instead I have to watch others do things for him that I can't.

I'm confident my child knows how much I love him. He's good about confiding in me about what's happening. But I want to act more strongly on his behalf.

Help me see that my prayers for him equate to front-line battling. Remove that helpless feeling I have, and shift my focus to Your strength. Remind me that I'm not powerless when Your Spirit is working through me.

I never was the one who protected and helped him; I know that. It was always You. I'm grateful that You used me sometimes, but everything good comes from You.

Now You have a new role for me in my child's life. Show me the value it has to him. Help me focus on what I can do, instead of what I can't do. Most of all, help me stay connected in a meaningful way to my child through this new season in his life. Amen.

After they prayed, the place where they were meeting was shaken. And they were all filled with the Holy Spirit and spoke the word of God boldly.

<small>ACTS 4:31 NIV</small>

Don't Let Me Be Jealous

Bitterness imprisons life; love releases it.

HARRY EMERSON FOSDICK

Dear Lord, I miss my child more than I ever thought I would. I know he's where he needs to be, but I want him back home. It's hard to see other parents with their kids close by when mine is so far away. I don't want to be jealous, but I am.

I know I'm being selfish. Help me change my attitude. I'm afraid it will bleed into the conversations I have with my child. I want him to feel my love and support without sensing any resentment for his choices.

Show me how to express my love and longing for him without making those around me uncomfortable. I need Your perspective on this. I need to once again feel pride and joy in the fact that he's making his own choices.

Don't let me drive away my friends with my jealousy. I am happy for them. Show me how to leave it at that and not continue into, *I just wish my child was home too.* You have a different path for each of us; help me be content with the one that's mine. Even more, help me be content with the one You have for my child. Amen.

Love is patient, love is kind. It does not envy, it does not boast, it is not proud.

1 CORINTHIANS 13:4 NIV

Help Me Know When to Let Them Fight Their Own Battles

If there exists no possibility of failure,
then victory is meaningless.

ROBERT H. SCHULLER

Dear Lord, please be with my child when he's in a situation that seems like more than he can handle. I want to help, but I'm torn. Help me know what to do.

My first impulse is to jump in and fix things. I have so much more experience when it comes to situations like this. But I got this experience by going through difficult times. If I rush in, am I denying him an experience he'll need later in life?

I know this is a time for him to practice standing on his own. But I don't want him to take on more than he can handle. If he doesn't get into things he can't handle alone, how will he ever learn to turn to You in all things? I'm so confused. Give me supernatural insight into when to step in and when to hold back and let You guide him.

Don't let me interfere with the lessons You have to teach him. I acknowledge that You want only the best for him. You are the One who knows the struggles that will refine him into the man of God he can become. Help me wait with faith until You call me to his side. Amen.

*"My sheep hear My voice,
and I know them,
and they follow Me."*

JOHN 10:27 NASB

Learning to Curb My Instincts

For the Spirit God gave us does not make us timid,
but gives us power, love and self-discipline.
2 TIMOTHY 1:7 NIV

When our boys were young, I often wondered what had possessed God to gift me with three of them. Growing up, it had only been me and one sister. I frequently reminded God that I wasn't cut out for the job of raising sons. Looking back on those conversations with Him, I can see Him in my mind's eye, smiling. His equipping came when I needed it, not in advance. I finally realized this one average morning as I got ready for the day.

Our youngest child was still a toddler, so after the other two left for school, I kept him in our bathroom with me while I finished curling my hair and putting on makeup. He was playing around the large empty garden tub, giggling and banging away with the toys I kept there, so I wasn't paying too close attention to what he was doing. In the next minute he was tugging at my skirt. "Look. Doggy, Mommy, doggy."

I turned to see the most miserable gecko I'd ever beheld clutched tightly in his fist. I couldn't scream for fear he'd squeeze too hard, with obvious tragic consequences. Instead I took a deep breath, whispered a prayer, and smiled at my proud toddler. I don't remember the words I used to keep him happy as I led him to the back door to let his "doggy" go out and play, but they worked. He released his new friend back into the wild, while inside I had a quiet nervous breakdown.

Later that evening, as I reflected on the events of the day, it occurred to me that if God had given me the strength and presence of mind to avert disaster in this minor happening, how much more would He equip me for the big things in their lives.

It's turned out to be true. When they've done things that made me want to scream—for various reasons—that's when I take a deep breath and turn to God, and I always have the strength I need.

Oceans of Life

You rule over the surging sea;
when its waves mount up, you still them.
PSALM 89:9 NIV

When the boys were young, we loved spending time at the beach. One of the first times all of the boys were big enough to get a little deeper into the ocean was a great conversation starter. We'd taken floats and the three boys out past the breaking waves just offshore. There they'd taken turns being pitched by their dad into the water, diving for sand dollars, and generally enjoying the deeper—calmer—ocean.

It had been a great afternoon, and as we sat around the table after supper that night, they started talking about the experience. There were amazed at the difference in the water as they'd managed to push past the crashing waves that threatened to knock them off their feet and the gentle swells as they got into deeper water.

My wise husband immediately jumped in and shared a life lesson. He reminded them that although we wouldn't always be with them, God would. We all face a lot of waves in life, but pushing through is always worth it. He pointed out that when we walk along the shore and look into the vast ocean of God's will, it's beautiful, but daunting. When we're afraid to commit ourselves one way or the other and stand in the rough surf, we're pounded by waves from every direction, not able to judge the situation accurately. But when we commit completely, pushing through to the deep, and immerse ourselves in God, we're gently cushioned and rocked, surrounded by His love and able to see the world from His point of view.

That lesson has stood me in good stead as I've watched our boys conquer the ocean of life, knowing that even when I couldn't be with them, God could.

Stepping Out
of Our Comfort Zone

{ *Because you know that the testing of your faith*
produces perseverance. }

JAMES 1:3 NIV

Two of our three boys are extroverts. They're comfortable around people they don't know and don't even mind speaking or performing. Our youngest child is the exact opposite. He's always struggled with shyness, and having two outgoing older brothers didn't always help the situation. But one of the things I admire most about this child is his willingness to stretch and grow.

He managed that growth in one unexpected area, though. He's still quite a legend at our local high school when it comes to the way a young man asked his date to prom.

He'd been agonizing for a little over a week about how he would invite this particular young woman to their junior/senior prom. The method he chose has yet to be topped. I heard the story after school that day.

All the teachers and office workers loved our child, and he'd managed to capitalize on that fact. He'd convinced one of them to let him ask his chosen date to prom during the school-wide announcements. Yep, my shyest child got on the loudspeaker at a high school of over 1,200 students and laid it all out for the girl of his dreams.

I have my own comfort zone, and it involves having my kids close by my side. But as I've watched how he's pushed himself to step out of his comfort zone, I've been encouraged to do the same, trusting God that He'll keep my boys safe when I'm not around. Just like our child built confidence on small successes and now even occasionally speaks to groups, I'm following his lead. His willingness to put his faith in God instead of his own abilities helps me refocus my own efforts.

Parenting Without a Parachute

Now to Him who is able to do far more abundantly beyond all that we ask or think, according to the power that works within us.

EPHESIANS 3:20 NASB

Sometimes—more often than not—I get caught up in the process of life. I'm an analytical sort of person, and I'm definitely a planner. Every project—parenting or otherwise—that I tackle involves planning. I try to anticipate any possible potholes and pitfalls. I build time lines and set expectations.

I'm also a recovering perfectionist.

For years I didn't realize I was a perfectionist. My perfectionism shows itself in strange ways. In the past it has kept me from trying anything I thought I couldn't succeed at. I've let it inhibit me as a parent. For me, failure wasn't an option, especially in the parenting arena. I wasn't going to be a parent responsible for messing up my kids' lives. That goal translated into a hurdle that kept me from moving forward.

In the past I've gone to great lengths to build in safeguards that keep failure at bay. I always thought of these things as like packing a parachute. I "packed a lot of parachutes" for my kids as they left my side. I thought of them as portable safety nets that would keep us from crashing and burning—if I hadn't covered all the possibilities.

Then one day I felt a metaphoric tap on the shoulder from the Holy Spirit. He asked me a question I've never forgotten.

Are you flying or skydiving?

You see, God is in the business of helping us to fly. He's not interested in skydiving, and He has no need of parachutes. Sure, there are things we need to do to get ready to fly, but packing a parachute isn't one of them. God wants us—and our children—to fly free, living the life He's planned for us. His plan doesn't include the encumbrances of safety nets and parachutes. When He's in control, they're just extra baggage that can hold us tethered to the ground.

Parenting Minefields

If we are faithless, He remains faithful,
for He cannot deny Himself.
2 TIMOTHY 2:13 HCSB

Even though I'm a Christ-follower, I must admit I've always struggled with a specific aspect of parenting. What parts of the world do I allow my kids to be exposed to, and what parts do I label as off-limits? Do I let them watch television, movies, or go to public school? The list of decisions goes on and on. Beyond that, how do I enforce these boundaries when my kids are out of my control?

As parents, when we come face-to-face with these decision points, we find ourselves in a barren landscape full of land mines. The truth I've found is that there's no one right path through these decisions. Parenting isn't a one-size-fits-all proposition.

The way we make it through this minefield without casualties is to walk closely with God. Exposing one child to a certain situation will make them stronger, while exposing a different child to the same situation can derail them for years. To make matters worse, we as parents don't always have the insight to predict the outcome. And sometimes it just doesn't matter because our kids are going to be exposed anyway.

So what did I decide to do?

I chose to step out in faith, believing that God would equip me as I walked through the dangers of parenting. Beyond that, I believed that God was big enough to counteract any mistakes I made. I didn't always succeed; there were times I thought I knew best and life exploded around me. But God's faithfulness doesn't depend on my abilities.

The only thing I do know is that they do happen. I can relax—to a certain extent—and spend my energy on sticking close to God and leaving the navigating to Him.

IT'S OKAY TO FAIL.

None of us is perfect, not as parents and not as kids. By being willing to share our failures with our kids, we have the opportunity to teach them so much. This kind of transparency is particularly important when our kids are away from us. It's easy to keep up a front of perfection, but when we're willing to be vulnerable, we grow closer.

Our failures give our kids reasonable standards by which to judge themselves. Perfection is hard to live up to. We also are more approachable if we're authentic. Kids know that no one—not even a parent—is perfect. We actually give value to deception if we don't acknowledge our own shortcomings.

PARENT WITH AUTHORITY AND GENTLENESS.

We have each been chosen as the parent of a specific child by God Himself. We can rest in the assurance that He knows we are exactly what that child needs in a parent. That is a solid authority to base our parenting from. It's hard to remember when our kids are away from us, but that doesn't make it less important.

However, that isn't an excuse to be mean or heartless. We must use that authority as our foundation and confidence to give us the freedom to parent with gentleness and love.

DON'T LET SOCIETY DICTATE YOUR PARENTING STYLE.

Parenting styles come and go almost as quickly as fashion. What's accepted as necessary one year will be brushed off as frivolous the next.

Our basis of right and wrong must remain founded on God's Word. We must guard against the world's ever-changing interpretation of Truth. As the world around us rushes to tolerance and a frightening reframing of the Bible, we will find ourselves holding on for dear life.

Our kids live in the world. Many attend public schools or colleges. They will be inundated with worldly views, and we must have a solid foundation for the beliefs we hold to be true.

Chapter Five

A Foundation of Faith

The world we live in now is an ever-changing slide into chaos. The only hope of steadiness our kids have is in a firm foundation of faith. When we give them that gift, they're able to meet whatever challenges come their way.

Help My Child Make His Faith His Own

Each day of our lives we make deposits
in the memory banks of our children.

CHARLES R. SWINDOLL

Dear Lord, how grateful I am to know You and know the love You have for me. But I want—more than anything—for my child to have that assurance. I know that he knows the truth, but he's in the process of making his faith his own, and it's hard to watch him struggle.

Dig Your truth out of his heart and let him see it clearly. When doubts arise, show him plainly what is a lie and what is not. I know he's going to be exposed to a lot of different viewpoints as he grows up. Cement a desire in his heart to investigate all he hears. I know that You will reveal Yourself to him when he searches.

Most of all, protect him from anyone who would mislead him. Lord, I know You love him even more than I do. Let me rest in that knowledge. Amen.

The Lord is not slow about His promise, as some count slowness, but is patient toward you, not wishing for any to perish but for all to come to repentance.

2 PETER 3:9 NASB

Replace My Child's Fear with Faith

> The greatest mistake we make is living
> in constant fear that we will make one.
>
> JOHN C. MAXWELL

Dear Lord, please be with my child when he is fearful. I don't understand why this is happening, and I know he doesn't either. But I know You're there with him, and I'm trying to keep moving ahead in faith. I'm praying that You would replace my child's fear with faith.

Don't allow him to be overwhelmed by circumstances. You promise to be everything we need. Show my child the truth of that promise right now, right where he is. Use the struggles in his life to illustrate how much You love him. Grow his faith to meet every situation he could encounter. You are worthy of our faith. Remind him just how trustworthy You are.

I've always trusted You to be everything I need. I admit it's harder to trust You to be everything my child needs, though— especially when he's away from me. I am choosing to have faith in You for my child's welfare. Give him the same peace that I have when I turn everything over to You. Amen.

When I am afraid,
I will trust in You.
PSALM 56:3 HCSB

Teach My Child That Your Will Is a Safe Place

The safest place in all the world is in the will of God,
and the safest protection in all the world is the name of God.

WARREN WIERSBE

Dear Lord, there are a lot of things happening in my child's life right now. Through it all, I have confidence that she's seeking Your will and purpose for her life. Show her there's nothing to fear from situations when she follows You.

Though there will be times when her life may seem like nothing but chaos, give her Your refuge of peace. Show her that being safe has nothing to do with physical or even emotional safety, but it comes from walking closely with You.

The world will try to convince her that following You is dangerous. Prepare her for this battle. Put people in her life who will fight alongside her. Give her friends to pray with. Surround her with godly mentors and champions.

I want to be there to fight for her, but I have to do my fighting here on my knees. I know that when she is with You, she is safe—eternally safe. That gives me peace when I feel overwhelmed. Give her that same reassurance as she turns to You. Set Your angels around my child to stand between her and those who would lead her astray. You are all she needs; remind her of this when life seems hopeless. Amen.

Even though I walk through the darkest valley, I will fear no evil, for you are with me; your rod and your staff, they comfort me.

PSALM 23:4 NIV

Give My Child a Hunger for You

May God so fill us today with the heart of Christ
that we may glow with the divine fire of holy desire.

A. B. SIMPSON

Dear Lord, as my child grows, I'm asking for You to give her an unquenchable hunger and thirst for You. She has a foundation of faith, but I know it's time for her to make her own decisions about what she believes.

Surround her with others who are hungry for You. Spur them on to learn more about You together. Remind me that even if it seems like she's on the wrong path, I know her search for truth will lead her to You.

Lord, Your Word is truth, and I'm asking You to make that foundational to who she is. Give her older, wiser companions who can help her sort out the truth from lies. Offer her opportunities to read the Bible and learn more about Your character.

When she questions what she sees, make sure she has people around her who will offer wisdom from You. As she grows, her questions become harder to answer. Remind her that when she walks with You, she knows the One who knows all the answers. Amen.

God, You are my God;
I eagerly seek You. I thirst for
You; my body faints for You
in a land that is dry, desolate,
and without water.

PSALM 63:1 HCSB

Give My Child Opportunities to Grow in Faith

To learn strong faith is to endure great trials. I have learned my faith by standing firm amid severe testings.

GEORGE MÜLLER

Dear Lord, while my child is away, give him opportunities to grow in faith. As I envision his future, I'm fearful about what may lie before him, especially when he's away from my care. But I acknowledge that his safety doesn't come from being physically close to me; it only comes from being spiritually close to You.

So I'm once again turning my child over to You. Give him the spiritual insight he needs to see You at work around him. Help him be courageous as he stands up for what is right, instead of accepting the status quo. Show him when to stay and take a stand and when to leave a difficult situation.

I know there are times when he'll feel alone. Put people in his life to stand with him. Give him the specific victories and defeats he needs to grow stronger. Pull him closer to You, so that You're the first person he turns to in the good times and in the bad. Amen.

Consequently, faith comes from hearing the message, and the message is heard through the word about Christ.

ROMANS 10:17 NIV

Give My Child Peace in the Midst of Chaos

> Faith is the strength by which a shattered world
> shall emerge into the light.
>
> HELEN KELLER

Dear Lord, please be with my child when he finds himself in the middle of chaos. I know he can be overwhelmed by circumstances and emotions. I want to be there with him, but that's just not always possible.

Help him sort through everything that's going on right now. Give him the ability to slow down, look beyond how he feels, and act on what he knows is true. You have given him a firm foundation; now show him how to apply what he's learned.

Bring him people who will speak truth and encouragement to him. Give him order and options. What he needs is constructive help to find his way through.

Make sure he's not alone or feeling abandoned. Keep me—and others—from overwhelming him with phone calls and suggestions. Put a guard on my mouth so I only have things to say that will point him to Your path through this.

Surround him with people who will be praying for him, and will pray with him. More than anything, he needs to stay connected to You, God. Protect him from anything or anyone who would pull him away. Amen.

Give all your worries to him, because he cares about you.

1 PETER 5:7 NCV

Help My Child
Recognize Deception

The first point of wisdom is to discern that which is false;
the second, to know that which is true.

LUCIUS CAELIUS LACTANTIUS

Dear Lord, give my child discernment to tell truth from lies. Don't allow her to doubt everything she knows to be true.

Intervene in her life. Show up in a powerful and recognizable way. Bring people to her who can help her sort out what's happening. Give her the insight she needs to see when she's being manipulated. Bring people of good character and integrity into her life.

Don't let her be pulled deeper and deeper in by those who would deceive her. Remind her of what she knows is true. Help her compare those truths to what she is being told by those who would deceive her. Strengthen her ties with You so she can heed Your Spirit's nudging. Don't abandon her in the camp of the enemy. Rescue her and bring her back into the safety of Your will. Amen.

Therefore, dear friends, since you know this in advance, be on your guard, so that you are not led away by the error of lawless people and fall from your own stability.

2 PETER 3:17 HCSB

Lend My Child Your Perspective

Don't let obstacles along the road to eternity
shake your confidence in God's promise.
The Holy Spirit is God's seal that you will arrive.

DAVID JEREMIAH

Dear Lord, my child needs Your perspective as she grows. Our world is complex, confusing, challenging, and often very hard. During those times when she is most confused, pick her up and shed Your light on what's happening.

When she's overwhelmed, remind her that everything that she experiences needs to be filtered through Your truth. Bring Bible verses to her mind that help her do that. Start now to build that foundation inside her so it's there when she needs it.

Begin now to put people in her life who are strong believers. Give her friends who are rooted and grounded in Your truth. Help them all see through the lens of Your love, Your truth, and Your holiness.

We know the Bible tells us that You work all things together for good. Continue to grow her faith as she refocuses on You. When bad times come, never let her forget that none of it took You by surprise and that You are with her always. Give her the faith and strength to know that You are always with her. Amen.

So we fix our eyes not on what is seen, but on what is unseen, since what is seen is temporary, but what is unseen is eternal.

2 CORINTHIANS 4:18 NIV

Grow My Faith

The beginning of anxiety is the end of faith,
and the beginning of true faith is the end of anxiety.

GEORGE MÜLLER

Dear Lord, sometimes I look at the bad things that could happen and am not good at focusing on the positive. Help me when it seems that the bad things I worried about are all coming to pass.

Help me to have faith during this time. Show me the blessings that are always present in our lives. In every circumstance, please grow my faith.

Sometimes my faith is so small. I didn't even realize it, but I have often tackled life in my own strength. Lord, I'm out of strength. Lord, lend me Your strength when I have none of my own.

You are my only hope. I seem to have lost my strong foundation of active faith to hold on to. But I'm choosing to believe You will give me one. Restore my trust, even as You grow my faith.

Lord, just as my child needs me to be strong, I need to know that You are there for me. Let me be an example of how even now I need to come to You and seek Your help so that my child will know that is what we can always do, especially when I have baby faith and what I need is hero faith. Show me that even a small grain of faith is enough as long as we hold on to You. Amen.

Immediately the father of the boy cried out, "I do believe! Help my unbelief."

MARK 9:24 HCSB

My Heart Is Breaking Because My Child Has Been Taken from Me

Trust the past to God's mercy, the present to God's love,
and the future to God's providence.

AUGUSTINE

Dear Lord, my heart is breaking. Do You understand what I'm feeling? You gave Your child up, but mine has been wrenched away, pulled out of my life without my consent. I need Your strength right now. Give me the peace I so desperately need.

You are my Rock and my Sustainer. Help me trust You with this situation. Guide everyone now in my child's life and make certain they don't stand in the way of Your will for his life.

The words of the Bible run through my mind, reminding me that You love him more than I do. Show me what that looks like in our lives and remind me that You are standing guard over every aspect of His life. Show me ways that I can still impact his life and have a significant place in it.

Even if I don't see that confirmation in a tangible way, help me stay strong and believe it anyway, simply because You promised it. Grow my faith through this, but even more, grow his. Become real to him in ways I couldn't even imagine. Remind me that You are still the One in control. You are our foundation, so help us choose to stand on You and You alone. Amen.

But I will sing about your strength. In the morning I will sing about your love. You are my defender, my place of safety in times of trouble.

PSALM 59:16 NCV

Teach Me to Trust You with My Child

Faith never knows where it is being led,
but it loves and knows the One who is leading.

OSWALD CHAMBERS

Dear Lord, I'm a little short on trust now that my child is away from home more and more. I'm ashamed to admit it, but it's true and I need help. I thought I trusted You, but now I realize I have a long way to go.

I see now that I was relying on my own strength to keep my child safe. Help me see the truth—that You and only You are the One who protects my child. Remind me of all the times You have already intervened in his life.

Now I'm relying on You completely to keep him safe. Looking back, I see that You do have him safely in Your hands, even when he's out of mine. You can prompt others nearby to help him when he needs it. Don't let me forget that.

Show me some of the ways You're providing for him. I know I shouldn't need this extra comfort, but I do. Help me let go of the stress and worry. I can't accomplish anything by hanging on to those things. You are all I need. More than that, I'm standing on the fact that You are all my child needs. Amen.

Many are the woes of the wicked, but the LORD's unfailing love surrounds the one who trusts in Him.

PSALM 32:10 NIV

Don't Let My Self-Worth Be Determined by My Child's Choices

God is love. He didn't need us. But he wanted us.
And that is the most amazing thing.
RICK WARREN

Dear Lord, my child isn't always going to make perfect choices. When he chooses badly, don't let me feel like a failure as a parent. I've tried to give him a foundation of faith, but I know that isn't always going to be enough when temptation strikes.

Stop me when I fall into the trap of comparing my child to other kids. I know things can appear very different when looking from the outside in. Help me to always stand firm in the knowledge that You've been with me throughout all my parenting choices—good and bad.

Don't let me take ownership of my child's choices. Protect me from allowing my self-worth to be tied up with his performance. This isn't Your truth. Don't let me fall for that lie. Help me recognize this struggle in other parents and offer them encouragement.

Let me see the things I've done wrong and ask forgiveness for them. Then show me how to walk away and leave them behind. I know that my child is now making his own decisions, and whatever they are, You're still in control. Amen.

"The LORD your God is with you; the mighty One will save you. He will rejoice over you. You will rest in his love; he will sing and be joyful about you."
ZEPHANIAH 3:17 NCV

What's in a Name

{ *"Do not fear, for I have redeemed you;*
I have called you by name; you are Mine!" }

ISAIAH 43:1 NASB

I never realized how important a name was until the year our middle child began work at summer camp. It was a camp all our sons had grown up attending. One of the things they loved most about it was the fact that each counselor had a cool name and a story to go with how he'd gotten it.

The counselors—new and returning—started the summer several weeks before the campers arrived. There was a lot of work to be done to get things ready for the season, and most important of all, the new counselors had to earn their names. Truthfully, I think this is one of the things our child was most excited about when he was hired to work at this camp. Each year, one of the new counselors is given a name of honor containing the silent *K*. Our child's goal was clear—earn *that* name.

Sure enough, on his first visit home he announced the fact that he'd won his name and was now known as Hakunak (pronounced *Hakuna*). I'm glad I didn't know until after the fact how he earned it. He was so excited to share his adventures with us. From climbing, to working the hardest, and even to eating a few bugs, he'd let nothing stand in his way. I shuddered as I listened, but the pride on his face kept me from voicing my concerns. They were worthless anyway; he'd come through his adventures unscathed. As always, God had taken care of him.

With God, we don't have to go to great lengths and sacrifices to earn our names. It was Jesus who did the sacrificing so we could be reconciled with the One who loves us most. He calls each of us—parents and children—by name, proving to everyone how important we are to Him.

What If—Not a Place
for Parents to Dwell

*"For I know the plans I have for you"—this is
the LORD's declaration—"plans for your welfare,
not for disaster, to give you a future and a hope."*
JEREMIAH 29:11 HCSB

Several years ago, our family had quite a scare. Our youngest child was back home from college and at a trampoline park with friends. He landed wrong and broke his back. Fortunately there was no spinal cord damage.

I'm good in a crisis. For some reason the situations that cause other people to panic create in me to the ability to act clearly and decisively. So when they brought him home, I was woman-in-control. I can be calm and clearheaded in the worst catastrophe.

At least until the crisis is over.

Then I fall apart—sometimes for several days. The slightest thing will bring uncontrollable sobs. It's all because after everything is said and done, I decide to take up residence in the place of *what-if*.

We've all been there, caught in the unending loop of shoulda, woulda, coulda. We replay scenarios, letting our minds wander from bad to worse.

If the break had been one millimeter to the left or the right.

If we hadn't gone ahead and taken him to the emergency room.

If there had been swelling.

Those dark places of what-if are populated with nightmares

of our own imaginings. But this isn't a place where parents need to go. We are protected from the horrors of what-if by an all-seeing God. He never sleeps, and He never relaxes His vigilance on our behalf.

This doesn't mean bad things won't happen—far from it in this world. *But* we have His promise that He will take those tragedies and turn them into good. He has our future well in hand.

So when you're tempted to vacation in the *Land of What-If*—especially when your child is away from your side—take a deep breath, look up, and choose to dwell in the land of certainty. It's a place of welfare, not disaster, and it's filled with hope.

Faith of a Headless Horseman

{ *The heart is more deceitful than anything else,*
and incurable—who can understand it?
JEREMIAH 17:9 HCSB }

We love fall at our house. Living in the foothills of the Blue Ridge Mountains gives us a gorgeous autumn. Everywhere we look, evidence of the season jumps out at us. The trees have donned their colorful best, and pumpkins are sprouting grins on every front porch. Halloween candy is littering the aisles at the grocery store, and kiddos are planning costumes. Along with this, we can pull out some classics to enjoy as a family, from *It's the Great Pumpkin, Charlie Brown* to *The Legend of Sleepy Hollow*.

It's that classic book—or more specifically, a character in that short story by Washington Irving that long ago caught my mind's eye with a spiritual application. As I was watching a rerun of Disney's version with my boys, I was struck by how we often resemble the Headless Horseman when it comes to faith.

The truth is, sustaining faith is based on facts, *not* feelings. When I follow my heart—what feels right—I lose touch with the head of my faith. My emotions really run away with me when I'm worried about my kids. I can envision so many catastrophes—especially when they're away from home—that I find myself fighting outright panic.

During those times when I'm fearful about my children, I have to remind myself that God is a God of concrete facts. He is the head of my faith. *That's* my strong foundation.

Fact one, God is always true to His Word. His faithfulness

about keeping my kids safe rests with Him, not with anything I do or don't do. Some days I stumble. I make wrong choices. I'm overwhelmed with guilt. But the truth is that God's promise don't rely on me. They're predicated on *His* goodness and mercy.

Fact two, God loves me . . . no matter what, and even more than that, He loves my children. His love promises He will never leave us nor forsake us. He is always there by my side, and He is always with my kids.

Fact three, God works all things together for good for those who love Him and are called to His purpose. When we look around, we see a world in a mess. Everything is upside down. Bad things happen to good people, and good things happen to bad people. The thought of the injustice in the world coming against my kids, fills me with terror. But I've learned that when I'm overwhelmed, I need to narrow my focus to God. He's the One who brings things back to good. We can't know in advance how God ties up all the threads and finishes off the tapestry. But we can rest in the truth that He does.

So again I say, *Faith is based on fact, not feelings*. This time the words come with confidence and with gratitude. I am a woman filled with fears for my kids. When I'm swayed by those emotions, I can end up like the Headless Horseman, cutting down people on all sides as I flounder through life trying to protect them while blind. When I let God take back being the head of my life, I'm protected from whims of feelings. His truth is certain, enduring for eternity.

Living in the Future

No, dear brothers and sisters, I have not achieved it,
but I focus on this one thing: Forgetting the past and
looking forward to what lies ahead, I press on to reach
the end of the race and receive the heavenly prize
for which God, through Christ Jesus, is calling us.

PHILIPPIANS 3:13–14 NLT

Parenting is one of the toughest things we'll ever have to do. It's almost impossible to make any decision without feeling like you're throwing your heart into a lions' den. Past mistakes crowd forward in our minds, issuing dire warnings and predictions of failure.

This is especially true when our kids are out of our sight. We wonder if we've equipped them fully, if our decision has led them into disaster, if they'll heed the warnings we've issued.

With a mind focused on past mistakes, it's possible to feel like we've shriveled up and died. We can get so overwhelmed with failure that we decide to stop moving at all. We can fall into the trap of feeling like anything we do is wrong, so why bother.

It's easy to become overwhelmed with doubt, insecurity, and an almost overwhelming urge to give up. Instead, draw a line in the sand. Commit today, *right now*, to begin to live in the future, on the promises God has given you. God has promised us—and that includes our kids—a future, a hope, and a calling. But we must let our children walk into that future. We won't always be there to protect them, but God will, and He is faithful.

God has called each of us to an amazing journey. It will be punctuated with highs and lows, but He has equipped you for the parenting road ahead. Now it's time to move forward, believing that God truly is big enough to make it happen. He doesn't call us out, fully formed and ready. He calls us out when we're weak—ready for Him to equip us.

My Wait Problem

> *The LORD is good to those who wait for Him,*
> *to the person who seeks Him.*
> LAMENTATIONS 3:25 NASB

Even though my parenting journey has, at times, seemed like twenty years spent on a speeding raceway, during those years there was a great deal of waiting involved. From waiting for them to come home from school to waiting for them to come back from a trip, for me waiting equaled worry. I must own that I am not a patient person anyway—and I am a control freak—so patience was a struggle.

But God showed me that He works in the waiting. It was during those hours of worry and fretting that He taught me to trust Him. He proved over and over again that He was trustworthy as He kept my kids safe when they were away from my side.

We think of waiting as this thing we must to do to reach what we want—in this case, my kids back safe at home. Truthfully, what we want is being accomplished *as we wait.*

Waiting isn't a static barrier we must burst through to reach the results we're waiting for—it's the vehicle we board to make the trip.

So make the same kind of adjustment I had to make. Look at waiting as an active process. Ask for new eyes to see what's really happening around and through you. Then rejoice in the journey, as God uses waiting to bring everyone back home, safe and sound.

ALWAYS PRAY FIRST.

This is my one hard and fast parenting rule for myself. As my kids spent more and more time away from home, it became more and more important. I start my day with prayer, my meals with prayer, and every single parenting decision with prayer.

Sometimes the prayers are more in the vein of distress flares shot toward heaven, but it's the fact I'm praying that's important. It gives me confidence to be reminded that I'm not in this alone and I'm not the ultimate authority.

Internally whispered prayers have saved me from speaking before I thought. Prayers shared with my kids before we drive off, remind them that God is always available, no matter how trivial the situation may seem. I cannot imagine a single instance when praying first won't make things better—instantly.

BE WILLING TO WAIT.

Parenting is a long-haul endeavor. Children don't grow up overnight—even if it sometimes seems that way. While we've all heard the joke about *not* praying for patience, this is the time when we need it the most.

We must be willing to be patient with ourselves as much as with our kids. Parenting is hard work, and we're bound to mess up along the way. We can't live in our failures. We must pick ourselves up and move on. God will work in us for change, just like He's at work in our kids. But this kind of change takes years, not days.

Sometimes we give and give and give and it's not until years later that we see the end result. God has an eternal perspective, and as parents, we need to cultivate that view as well.

DON'T BASE YOUR SELF-ESTEEM ON YOUR KIDS.

We are precious because of who we are to God, not what we do, and certainly not what our kids do. Every child makes mistakes, chooses wrongly, and occasionally goes off the rails. If we base our worth on our kids, we are setting ourselves up for failure.

Our children's mistakes aren't grades given on some parenting report card. God chose us as much for the mistakes He knows we'll make as for the things right we'll do. He alone sees how the things in our kids' lives will shape them into men and women who love Him.

Chapter Six

A Core
of Strength

Children are so often more resilient than we give
them credit for. But beyond that natural inclination,
we have a responsibility to instill in them a core of
strength of who they are in God.

Let My Child See Your Truth

Everything deep is also simple and can be reproduced simply
as long as its reference to the whole truth is maintained.
But what matters is not what is witty but what is true.

ALBERT SCHWEITZER

Dear Lord, be with my child when he is in a new situation. He's having to process so much information and make decisions he's never had to make before. Use this time to teach him how to discern Your truth about everything around him.

In our world today, it's hard to tell good from evil. But when we go back to Your Word, the Bible gives us the foundation to know one from the other. Make sure my child has access to Your Word. Beyond that, give him a driving thirst to spend time every day reading the Bible and praying.

You have put Your Holy Spirit inside each of us who call You Lord. Help him follow the guidance of Your Spirit. Teach him to rely on You for direction in all his decisions.

Thank You for loving my child even more than I do. Show him that love by giving him supernatural insight into what's going on around him. I know some of the influences he's being exposed to are not from You. Protect him by arming him with Your truth.

Put others around him who also know Your truth. Bring them together and guard them from harm as they stand for Your principles. Amen.

*"Sanctify them in the truth;
Your word is truth."*

JOHN 17:17 NASB

Give My Child Everything She Needs

God always gives His best to those
who leave the choice with Him.

JIM ELLIOT

Dear Lord, the Bible tells us to pray, *Give us our daily bread*. Today I'm asking that You provide my child with her daily bread. I'm not always with her, so I can't be the one to provide for her. I worry that when we're separated, she won't have the things she needs.

Make sure that no matter where she is, those who are caring for her are also providing for her. I want her to have plenty to eat and the clothes she needs, but there's so much more I want for her. I want her to feel Your love and be reminded to read her Bible. I want her to have the opportunity to grow, in a safe and happy environment.

Use those around her to remind her how much You love her. Don't ever let her forget how much I love her too.

Give her the protection and encouragement that only You can provide. Let her feel Your presence as she goes through her day and lies down to sleep. Be her Provider and her Protector. Amen.

"Give us today our daily bread."
MATTHEW 6:11 HCSB

Give My Child Discipline and Perseverance

Pray as though everything depended on God.
Work as though everything depended on you.
AUGUSTINE

Dear Lord, my child is entering a new season of her life. She's building on the experiences she's had before, and I rejoice in the way I see her growing. I'm praying that as she grows she'll continue to develop discipline and perseverance in her life.

A lot of things have come easily for her, and I pray that ease won't become a stumbling block for her. Use this time to stretch and grow her into the young woman You would have her become.

When she faces things that are difficult, show her the core of strength that You have gifted her with. Remind her that her strength comes from You, and because of that, it's inexhaustible. Surround her with others who also know how to persevere.

Give her just enough obstacles to help her grow strong without becoming frustrated. Put friends in her life who will encourage her when things get tough. Let her see the rewards that come from pushing through to the other side of difficult times.

Show her the impact she can have in the lives of others when she keeps moving forward instead of giving up. Remind her that she never faces anything—easy or hard—without Your constant presence. Amen.

Let us not become weary in doing good, for at the proper time we will reap a harvest if we do not give up.
GALATIANS 6:9 NIV

Give My Child Courage

> Take courage. We walk in the wilderness today
> and in the Promised Land tomorrow.
>
> D. L. MOODY

Dear Lord, please help my child be brave. I know that she's fearful about a lot of things. Use this time to grow her courage. Show her that courage isn't the absence of fear, but continuing on in spite of the fear.

Put her in situations that provide her with opportunities to grow and blossom into the strong woman I know she is inside. Remind her that she never has to face anything alone. You are always with her. Give her insights that she can recognize as only having come from You.

As she's forced into uncomfortable situations, show her the joy that comes from facing her fears head-on. Let her see how her fears are sometimes a positive thing, keeping her from situations that could cause harm. Help her develop the instincts You've given her. Show her how You use that insight to keep her safe.

"Be strong and courageous, do not be afraid or tremble at them, for the LORD your God is the one who goes with you. He will not fail you or forsake you."

DEUTERONOMY 31:6 NASB

As she learns to follow You into places she never dreamed, help her give others courage. Finally, never let the what-ifs of life keep her from experiencing the joy You have planned for her. Amen.

Don't Let My Child Forget Who You Are

Worldliness is what makes sin look normal
in any age and righteousness seem odd.
DAVID F. WELLS

Dear Lord, my child is away from home more and more. As he makes new friends and begins to spread his wings, I'm scared he may drift away from the person we have raised him to be. I don't want him to forget the standards he was raised with.

No matter what else is going on, don't let him forget who You are. Use this time of new experiences to help him grow closer to You, instead of further away. Thank You for the way You've made sure he has the foundation he needs to build on.

He'll meet people who don't believe as he does. As he's exposed to new ideas, give him the wisdom to be able to tell the difference between Your truth and the ways of the world. Help him make wise decisions, even when they're not popular decisions.

Help him find friends who do have the same beliefs. Show them how to support one another, and don't let them be pulled away from Your truth. I know he's meeting new people and learning new things. Don't let them cause him to reject You or Your values. Amen.

Do not be misled:
"Bad company corrupts
good character."
1 CORINTHIANS 15:33 NIV

Help My Child During This Illness

You can't have healing without sickness.

T.D. Jakes

Dear Lord, my child is sick and I'm scared. He's away from me, and I want to be with him to take care of him. I know he doesn't feel well, but I know You have him in Your perfect care, even when I can't be there with him.

This physical challenge has caught him off guard. Not only does he feel bad, but this is disrupting his life. He's not used to struggling in this way. Please be present with him and give others around him a sense of understanding and patience while he recovers.

I'm also begging You to intervene for him. Give the doctors Your insight and wisdom so they know how to treat this. Guide them to the exact right treatment plan for his situation.

Put doctors and nurses around him who know You as the Great Physician. Don't let him receive poor care or bad advice. Protect him from all who would make this situation worse.

Please make him better through Your divine healing. Help him to recover more each day. Show both of us how You're working through this struggle, and grow our faith. Amen.

Bless the LORD, O my soul, and forget none of His benefits; Who pardons all your iniquities, Who heals all your diseases.

PSALM 103:2–3 NASB

Keep My Child Healthy

Wisdom is the power to see and the inclination
to choose the best and highest goal,
together with the surest means of attaining it.

J. I. PACKER

Dear Lord, keep my child healthy. There are so many ways that kids can get sick. Please protect her from viruses, bacteria, and things I don't even know about. Strengthen her body's defenses so she can stay strong.

Help her make wise choices when it comes to what she eats and drinks. Give her an awareness of her body and what it needs. Don't let her ignore the warnings she may feel. Provide her with plenty of opportunities for rest and sleep. Protect her from stress that could weaken her health.

Don't let her forget to turn to You when she struggles physically. Make sure she remembers that You are Lord over more than just the spiritual realm. Remind her of the comfort and insight You've provided her on other occasions.

As she goes about her days, trying new things, strengthen her intuition. When she's presented with choices, put people around her to help her choose wisely. When she is exposed to germs, protect her from getting sick. If she does get ill, make sure she has access to good medical care. Be her Caregiver when I can't be there with her. Amen.

*Therefore, brothers, by
the mercies of God, I urge you
to present your bodies as
a living sacrifice, holy and
pleasing to God; this is your
spiritual worship.*

ROMANS 12:1 HCSB

Give My Child a Heart to Encourage Others

The greatest blessing in the whole world is being a blessing.
JACK HYLES

Dear Lord, as much as I want my child to receive encouragement while he's away from home, I want him to offer encouragement to others as well. I've watched his gift to cheer others on grow and blossom.

Don't let him get self-focused and overwhelmed with his new circumstances. Let him see the people around him who need his help. Some of those he comes into contact with may be irritating and hard to like. Show him what's going on beneath the surface of their carefully crafted public mask.

Help him love the unlovable and reach out to those who are lonely. It's Your love that is inside him enabling him to encourage others. Use this new situation to define and focus that gift.

As he reaches out to others, I know he'll make mistakes. Don't let those missteps discourage him or make him fearful. Let those lessons lead to his wisdom as he grows into the man You have planned for him to become. Amen.

> *If one of you says to them, "Go in peace; keep warm and well fed," but does nothing about their physical needs, what good is it?*
> JAMES 2:16 NIV

Teach Me How to Pray

Strive in prayer; let faith fill your heart—so will you be strong in the Lord, and in the power of His might.

ANDREW MURRAY

Dear Lord, I need to know how to pray. My words seem lifeless and weak. I want to be able to pray with power and eloquence.

Sometimes, as a parent, I feel powerless. I know the Bible assures me that the strongest thing I can do is pray, but what if my prayers are weak? Will You still hear and respond?

Show me what it means to pray with confidence. I don't want to just read someone else's words. I want *my* words to rise to heaven.

Is my focus in the wrong place? Maybe it's not the words that bring the power, it's Your response. Remind me that You hear me no matter what. Help me to gain confidence, not in me and what I say, but in You.

Give me the courage to bring everything to You and not worry about how the words come out. Show me that nothing is too small to bring to You, especially concerning my child. You care about what I care about. You love my child more than I ever could. I'm choosing to believe that. I will rest in the fact that You hear every whisper of my soul and cry of my heart. Amen.

It happened that while Jesus was praying in a certain place, after He had finished, one of His disciples said to Him, "Lord, teach us to pray just as John also taught his disciples."

LUKE 11:1 NASB

137

Fill Me Up, I'm Empty

Every tomorrow has two handles. We can take hold of it
with the handle of anxiety or the handle of faith.

HENRY WARD BEECHER

Dear Lord, fill me up, I'm empty and unable to cope by myself.
As my child grows, she's away more and more. I find myself so
focused on my worries about her that I forget to trust You and
seek You first.

Restore my hope. Give me a reservoir of strength to pull
from. I'm tired of trying to do this on my own. I see now that this
is a situation that only You can solve.

I know You're faithful and that You love her even more than
I do. Show me how You're working in her life. I want to stand
strong on my faith because You are trustworthy.

My child is so beautiful and has such a bright future in front
of her. Don't let her throw it away for momentary happiness.
Remind her that choosing wisely
right now isn't the same as missing
out on something. Show her all that
You have for her. Amen.

*Be joyful in hope, patient in
affliction, faithful in prayer.*

ROMANS 12:12 NIV

Help Me Love My Child from a Distance

*It is not my ability, but my response
to God's ability, that counts.*
CORRIE TEN BOOM

Dear Lord, I feel like I have a pretty good handle on how to love my child when she was always at home. Now that she's away more and more, help me learn how to show my love for her in ways that mean the most to her. When we could spend time together, I didn't worry about making her feel loved. Now I feel so disconnected.

Boost my confidence as I learn some new parenting skills. I don't want to smother her or make her feel like I don't trust her. I also don't want her to think that when she's away, she's out of my thoughts. I need to find balance.

Put others in my life who have walked this path before. I could use some insight into how to navigate this new chapter in our lives. I think part of my worry is that I don't want to lose my place in her life. I've known this change was coming. I just didn't think it would be so difficult.

Help me view the changes with joy instead of sadness. Remind me that I'm not being replaced, but that she's putting into practice all she's learned. Help me take pride in the beautiful young woman she's becoming. Amen.

By helping each other with your troubles, you truly obey the law of Christ.
GALATIANS 6:2 NCV

Remind Me to Fight
on My Knees

Prayer is not conquering God's reluctance,
but taking hold of God's willingness.

PHILLIPS BROOKS

Dear Lord, while my child was at home all the time, I prayed for him daily, in addition to spending time with him. Now that he's away from home more, I confess that my prayers have become more like an afterthought. Remind me of how important those prayers truly are.

I'm learning that I can battle most effectively for my child—whether he's here or away—when I'm on my knees. In this position, I can ask for his protection, against anything and anyone. I can also pray for him to do well in his studies and have the mind of Christ as he struggles to retain all that he's learning in school.

You are with me as I call upon Your angels to guard him, keeping him physically safe in a dangerous world. Your Spirit helps me know when to pray for him to refocus on You, as well as how to discern the truth of his current situation.

The gift of prayer is one I've taken for granted in the past, but no longer. Don't ever let me forget that Your power is found when we bow before You. Amen.

> "If you remain in me and my words remain in you, ask whatever you wish, and it will be done for you."
>
> JOHN 15:7 NIV

Staying Plugged In

> *Let us hold on to the confession of our hope*
> *without wavering, for He who promised is faithful.*
> HEBREWS 10:23 HCSB

I was fortunate to enter into my years of parenting with a solid foundation of faith. You might think that made me a strong mother, but like everyone else, the strength ebbed and flowed depending on whether or not I stayed plugged in to God. That particular illustration was brought home to me one day while my husband and were updating our child's room.

But first a little background. About a year previously, we'd begun having a problem with the lights in our house. For no apparent reason, they'd flicker and dim. This occurrence wasn't limited to one specific room, but seemed to affect the entire house.

It drove my electrical engineer husband nuts.

This was a matter of pride for him. When the brownouts began, he made it his life's work to discover the cause. He spent hours with the fuse box, investigating wires, and finally moving on to testing everything electrical in our home. All with no result. The brownouts continued until even he was finally forced to shrug his shoulders and admit defeat.

Then it was time for a face-lift in our child's room. I'd decided to rearrange the furniture and repaint. That meant we'd have to move everything out and prep the walls—not an easy task in a room with an active boy. We'd spent a good part of the day spackling, taping, and removing wall socket coverings. It was while removing the faceplate from the socket behind our child's bed that my husband finally discovered the problem.

At some point, our inquisitive child had decided it would be a good idea to force a penny into one of the plugs, just to see what happened. We still don't know how he managed it without electrocuting himself. He didn't see any interesting result, so he just left the penny there and forgot about it. But that small coin had been causing the brownouts and power drains throughout our home.

Our faith sometimes has the same problem. I've seen it happen in my life, and in the lives of our kids. We're going along pretty good, staying close to God, and then, without realizing the consequences, we insert something between us. It doesn't have to be a big thing, but it can interrupt the power of God flowing through our lives. As parents, we need to watch for those brownouts and power drains in the lives of our kids, especially when they're growing and away from home more and more. Those small interruptions between us and God can affect everyone.

Choosing to Live in Grace, Not Guilt

> So now, those who are in Christ Jesus are not judged guilty. Through Christ Jesus the law of the Spirit that brings life made you free from the law that brings sin and death.
>
> ROMANS 8:1–2 NCV

Parenting can bring with it a ton of guilt. If we let ourselves, we can live under the weight of what we should and shouldn't have done in regard to raising our kids. For years, that was the place I called home. Then one day, God broke through the wall of guilt I'd built around myself.

It had happened . . . again. I'd sworn I'd hold my temper, but one of my sons had stepped over the line and I'd lashed out in anger. I could see the hurt in his eyes as my words rained down on him. But I couldn't stop. Finally he ran out of the room, and I collapsed in tears. I'd promised them just last week that their mom would do better.

Failure washed over me as I cried out to God, promising again to do better, to be more careful. This wasn't the first time I'd confessed this weakness. I'd wrestled with this issue again and again.

What kind of a person was I that I'd fall so easily back into the middle of temptation? My repeated lapses made me wonder if I was even a believer.

Once again, I went to one of my sons to tell him how sorry I was for hurting him. I asked him for forgiveness and with a hug, he gave it. That day, the sun broke through. If my tiny child could forgive me again and again, I knew God could too.

That single revelation has given me confidence. Not in myself . . . never in me. But in God.

He was always there to pick me up when I fell, always waiting to extend grace and give me another go. I was the one who struggled with shame and condemnation. That condemnation *never* came from Him.

Oh, don't get me wrong. I know it hurt Him—as much as it hurt my boys—when I gave in to sin. But He didn't return that hurt with punishment. He returned it with patience, grace, and love. I discovered I couldn't out-sin His mercy.

Do I still struggle? Sadly, yes. It's even easier to fall into the trap of condemnation as my child grows and is away from home more. But I'm quicker to admit my failings, and less willing to listen to the false guilt that comes from my enemy. Satan may try to lash my soul with guilt, but God extends His shield of infinite grace, and I'm at peace.

The Art of Being Still

He says, "Be still, and know that I am God; I will be exalted among the nations, I will be exalted in the earth."

PSALM 46:10 NIV

When I added *parent* to my list of job descriptions, life took off at light speed. Instantly my days were filled to overflowing with the things I should be doing. As my kids grew, instead of diminishing, the list continued to grow. Somewhere in the list of what I needed to do, the art of being still fell to the wayside.

Occasionally I'd get a much-needed wake-up call as a small voice pleaded with me, "Mommy, won't you just sit down and play?" Those reminders helped me slow down and remember what was truly important. But as my kids grew and were away from home more and more, those requests diminished. It was up to me to keep my foundation with them strong.

One summer day, God gave me an illustration for this truth that I'll never forget.

It had been a great vacation. We'd spent a glorious seven days at the beach. There had been plenty of time for taking long walks, playing in the water, searching for shells. But some of the best times were spent just lounging in our beach chairs, feet in the sand.

One late afternoon, the sky mirrored the dusky blue of the ocean and the tide began to turn. As the encroaching waves washed over my feet, I noticed something cool. When each wave receded, in its wake was left a shallow film of water. It was so clear and so calm I could see my face in it. This image was erased and replaced over and over again as rushing waves crashed upon the shore.

Then, like an oft-repeated saying, the truth of this visual lesson began to penetrate.

God was reminding me that when I get busy, rushing from thing to thing, it becomes harder and harder for my life to clearly reflect Christ. But when I slow down, living by His rhythm, His image is visible in all aspects of my life.

Where do you find yourself right now? Caught in the pounding surf or taking time to refresh yourself in the calm waters that reflect the light of His Spirit?

Developing Independence

> *The mind of man plans his way,*
> *but the LORD directs his steps.*
> PROVERBS 16:9 NASB

Early on in my mothering career, I had a sort of mental job description. It wasn't something I'd verbalized, but it was definitely there. I saw it as my job to love, protect, and educate my sons. I would guide them in the paths that God had designed just for them. All with love and patience. Can't you hear the heavenly chorus that accompanied this admirable plan? Needless to say, reality reared its ugly head pretty quickly.

The day-to-day journey of mothering involved a lot less heavenly chorus and a lot more frustration. The challenges were made worse by a severe lack of patience on my end, caused in part by sleep deprivation and the innate ability of my sons to know my weaknesses and capitalize on them. I think the common euphemism would be *pushing my buttons*. At times these strong-willed little boys didn't just push them, they jumped up and down, stomping on them until I screamed for mercy.

I grew up in a much different family, with only a single sister, a mom, and a dad—no boys in sight. So my introduction to a houseful of men was abrupt, to say the least. My idea of excitement growing up involved a good book or a long walk. My sons measure excitement in adrenaline highs.

Sewing and knitting have always been things I enjoyed, so before each child was born I spent a lot of my nesting energy on building a suitable baby wardrobe. This included hand-knitted booties, lace and linen play suits, even some smocked overalls—according to my husband, none of which were suitable for normal boys.

I managed to overrule him . . . until the boys could talk. Then their wardrobe was dictated by their preferences. I still made their clothes, moving on to sturdy corduroy pants and boy-friendly T-shirts.

I tried to interest them in nature and the amazing world around them—that netted me a bucket full of frogs for a present. Yes, I still have nightmares about that one.

I even suggested arts and crafts. But I was less than thrilled when one summer they discovered a clay deposit on the creek that ran through our backyard. They became potters on the spot, digging out the clay with such diligence that by the end of the summer, I just gave up on laundry and threw out their clothes.

Yep, as you might have guessed, motherhood was a no-holds-barred dose of reality for me. God gave me my boys as a precious gift. It was a hard gift to accept at first. I felt so inadequate. At times, I longed for youngsters that I could more easily identify with. But I discovered that having these boys pulled out a strength and a joy that only God knew was inside me. The rough-and-tumble acceptance and love of three small boys was a perfect fit to who God had designed me to be.

Thankfully, once I'd opened my eyes and come to grips with what "normal" began to look like with three young sons, life became an absolute joy. Sometimes the joyful laughter held a tinge of hysteria, but I still counted it as all good. I wouldn't trade a moment of getting to hold my sons' hands as we all learned to exercise independence and grow closer to God.

Exercising Independence

{ *I will walk about in freedom,*
for I have sought out your precepts.
PSALM 119:45 NIV }

Although independence is healthy, it can, in my humble opinion, be taken just a wee bit too far. Leave it to our middle child to go there.

After child number two graduated from high school, he decided to spend the next year or so at our local community college and live at home—a decision that his father and I wholeheartedly approved of. But it was tough on him. He wanted—more than almost anything—to be independent. He absolutely hated coming to us for help with his finances.

When he was accepted to a small private college an hour away, he was ecstatic. But staying in the dorm just wasn't an option, not on his budget or ours. So he agreed to live at home the first semester until he could work out a different living arrangement. Unfortunately that didn't last long. His solution?

He outfitted his beat-up old Toyota 4Runner with a twin bed, storage, and various other necessities and moved out. The rest of that semester he lived in a parking lot near the school. He claimed it was perfect, because he could park at one end and be close enough to access the free Wi-Fi at a fast-food establishment. Before the semester was over, he even had his own hashtag #ManWhoLivesInTruck. My only comment to him was this . . . #MakesAMommaProud.

Truthfully, I was proud. Even though his creative independence looked different than I had hoped it would, I could see God's hand clearly in his life. I was learning that God could be trusted with my son, no matter what.

LET GOD BE GOD IN YOUR CHILD'S LIFE.

When our kids are away from us, we have a unique opportunity to allow them to learn to hear God and act on what He says. The hard part of this is that sometimes He's only talking to your child, not you. God may choose not to repeat to us what He's saying to our kids.

The best thing we can do is to also stay tuned in to God's voice in our hearts. He will nudge us when to move and let Him take over.

REJECTION IS OFTEN GOD'S PROTECTION.

It's hard to watch our kids deal with rejection, especially when we're not there with them. They flunk a test, don't make a team, or lose a friend. All these things can feel like a failure to a child—and to us. But we need to remember—and point out to our kids—that these events may have been proof of God's protection.

Sometimes God is protecting us from bad things that could happen, sometimes from getting hurt further down the road. He can even be protecting us from good things that could bring about bad character traits in us later.

REMIND THEM THAT LIFE ISN'T EASY.

That sounds callous, especially if they're away from home. But it's important for all of us to remember that life is hard.

Sometimes our perspective gets warped and we expect things to always go smoothly and turn out well. We all need to be reminded that's not the case. When we expect things to be difficult, we're more equipped to deal with the disappointments that will come.

We don't want to be negative or pessimistic, but we want to impart a realistic outlook to our kids when they're away from us. We will always emphasize the foundation of faith from which we live our lives. But that foundation doesn't guarantee us an easy life.

Chapter Seven

Companions
Matter

We all need people around us to encourage and support us, and kids are no different. One of our parenting tasks is to teach our children how to make good decisions about those they choose to invest in as friends, mentors, and mates.

Guard My Child's Marriage

There is no more lovely, friendly or charming relationship,
communion or company, than a good marriage.

MARTIN LUTHER

Dear Lord, it was You who ordained marriage. Now my precious
child has entered into this relationship for herself. Today I'm asking You to guard my child's love for her husband. Help her not
to grow weary through the years to come. There are times of incredible joy and equal times of sorrow. Show her how to let these
times feed the love in her marriage, not tear it apart.

Give her husband the ability to love my child no matter what
comes. Even more than that, give him the ability to show her that
love in ways she understands.

Thank You for sending her a life partner who does love her.
Keep temptation far from their paths. Remind them to look to
You during the good times and bad. Use the stressful times in
their marriage to pull them closer to You and closer to each other.

You have given them to each
other, so don't let anything I say
or do interfere in that relationship.
Protect them from my best intentions, and from the times when I
am acting selfishly. Put them on
Your path. Do whatever it takes to
keep their love intact for a lifetime.
Amen.

*However, each one of you
also must love his wife as he
loves himself, and the wife
must respect her husband.*

EPHESIANS 5:33 NIV

Surround My Child with Friends

Love is not affectionate feeling, but a steady wish for
the loved person's ultimate good as far as it can be obtained.

C.S. LEWIS

Dear Lord, today I'm asking You to surround my child with friends. She's going to have to make some new friends, and I know that isn't always easy. Help her to make wise choices as she chooses her companions. I hope her new friends have the same foundation of faith, but I know that most likely not all of them will. Help her be a witness to her new friends and for them to find, in her, a true, loving friend who loves Christ first.

Give her other girls to share her hopes and dreams with, as well as her fears and struggles. Bind them together with a common belief system. Help them to hold each other accountable as they take on this new journey together. Show her how to be a good friend. As she finds other girls to hang out with, don't let her tender heart lead her into unwise choices.

Teach her more about You through the lives of those close to her. As she continues to grow, give her opportunities to develop the talents You've given her. Most of all, make sure she keeps her relationship with You as the top priority, no matter what. Amen.

> And if someone overpowers
> one person, two can resist
> him. A cord of three strands
> is not easily broken.
>
> ECCLESIASTES 4:12 HCSB

Teach My Child to Be a Good Friend

If we truly love people, we will desire for them far more
than it is within our power to give them, and this will lead us
to prayer: Intercession is a way of loving others.

RICHARD J. FOSTER

Dear Lord, I'm praying that You will teach my child how to be a
good friend. Give her the ability to share her foundation of faith
and encourage those around her. She's growing up and making
her own decisions. As she finds new friends, help her remember
to stay true to who she is.

Lead her to friendships that will allow her to exercise her gift
of encouragement. Let her be the kind of friend that will bring
joy to those around her. Show her how to be open and trusting
without putting herself in harm's way.

Help her be a friend who will strengthen others. Show her
how important it is to be a friend who will speak the truth to
another. Don't let her try to be someone she's not just to please
someone else. Show her how to look beyond what's on the surface and deep into the hearts of
those You put in her path. Give her
insight and wisdom as she reaches
out. Be an active part of her life,
and make sure she's always aware of
Your presence. Amen.

*Therefore encourage one
another with these words.*

1 THESSALONIANS 4:18 HCSB

Don't Let My Child Substitute Friendships for a Relationship with You

> As long as you want anything very much,
> especially more than you want God, it is an idol.
>
> A. B. SIMPSON

Dear Lord, I'm glad that my child has found good friends where she is right now. I worry that as their friendships grow, they'll begin to turn to one another instead of You.

Show them how to grow their friendships without sacrificing intimate time with You. Make sure that when things happen, You're still the first one she turns to. She has always relied on You as her rock and her foundation. Don't let that change with her circumstances.

Help these new friends to encourage one another to a deeper relationship with You. Give them opportunities to hold one another accountable as they grow closer. Don't let temptation lead them away from You while they're away from home.

As they encounter new situations, remind them of their foundation. Don't let the excitement of new experiences pull them away from following Your path. When they do slip, don't let them get away with wrongdoing. Hold them close and whisper Your love and protection into their lives at every turn. Amen.

> They exchanged the truth about God for a lie, and worshiped and served created things rather than the Creator—who is forever praised. Amen.
>
> ROMANS 1:25 NIV

Help My Child Find a Church

When a Christian shuns fellowship with
other Christians, the devil smiles.
When he stops studying the Bible, the devil laughs.
When he stops praying, the devil shouts for joy.

CORRIE TEN BOOM

Dear Lord, while my child is away from home, I'm praying for You to lead her to a community of believers. I'm sure she's missing her friends, and I ask that You will guide her to a church family where she can find new friends and companions.

Please help her find a new church home. She needs a place where she's encouraged to grow and learn more about You. I want her to once again experience the sweetness of corporate worship.

Put people in her life who will guide her as she looks for that community. Make sure it's a place where she feels loved enough to share the things she's struggling with. Surround her with those who can encourage her even as they share Your truth with her.

Help her find the courage to open up, not just about the good things, but also about the stresses in her life. Let her learn more about You through the godly people You put in her path. Most of all, remind her how much You love her. Amen.

You should not stay away from the church meetings, as some are doing, but you should meet together and encourage each other. Do this even more as you see the day coming.

HEBREWS 10:25 NCV

Give My Child Closure for a Difficult Relationship

It is true that we may desire much more.
But let us use what we have, and God will give us more.

ADONIRAM JUDSON

Dear Lord, my child has had her first bad breakup and she's far from home. I want to be there for her—to wrap her in my arms and help her through this. I know You're with her, and I'm praying she feels Your presence.

Give her friends to talk to as she processes this difficult change. Help her see Your will in this. Don't let her give in to the what-ifs that can come after the end of a relationship.

As she begins to carve out new paths, lead her carefully. When she finds herself in places that hold memories, replace the painful ones with new memories. Show her the joy that can be found in being a single rather than a couple, and in the future, not only in the past.

Surround her with wise counsel—from mentors as well as friends. Give them the right words to say. Help them walk the thin line between enough sympathy so she feels loved, but not enough to allow her to stay in the pit of depression.

Don't let her second-guess what's happened. Shower her with Your peace, and give her the closure she needs to move forward. Amen.

"If anyone will not welcome you or listen to your words, leave that home or town and shake the dust off your feet."

MATTHEW 10:14 NIV

Give My Child a Strong Female Role Model

God is more interested in your future
and your relationships than you are.

BILLY GRAHAM

Dear Lord, now that my child is away from home more, she needs more than just me as a strong female role model. She needs women who can guide her along the path to becoming the person of God You intended her to be. As she experiences new things, she still needs guidance. I can do some of that, but I can't always know what's happening.

Give her a mentor who has a heart for You, to guide her safely through opportunities and challenges. Give this mentor a loving heart, and help her see how much my child needs someone. Make sure my child listens to Your Spirit when she decides whom to trust.

Remind her that while You are the One who directs her path, You often use people to reinforce that truth. Amen.

Plans fail when there is no counsel, but with many advisers they succeed.
PROVERBS 15:22 HCSB

Give My Child a Strong Male Role Model

At times our own light goes out and is rekindled by
a spark from another person. Each of us has cause
to think with deep gratitude of those
who have lighted the flame within us.

ALBERT SCHWEITZER

Dear Lord, as my child continues to grow into a young man, he needs more mature men in his life as role models. While he was home most of the time, he had that. Now I'm worried about who will try to fill that place in his life.

Help him be careful when he chooses whom to imitate and respect. Make sure the men in his life know You, Lord, and have a strong foundation of faith. Use Your Spirit to lead him to the person You have already picked out.

Please provide someone who knows, from Your example, the true characteristics of a godly man. Amen.

The things which you have heard from me in the presence of many witnesses, entrust these to faithful men who will be able to teach others also.

2 TIMOTHY 2:2 NASB

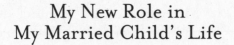

My New Role in My Married Child's Life

As God by creation made two of one,
so again by marriage He made one of two.

THOMAS ADAMS

Dear Lord, my child has chosen his wife. Although I'm joyful about this new life for my child, I still feel replaced. I have been replaced as the woman in his life, and I wouldn't want it any other way. But my heart is sad, because it's no longer me he comes to first. Teach me to rejoice in this new role.

You have given my child a beautiful lifemate. I've prayed for her since his birth, and this is the woman You have chosen to answer my prayers. Help me love her with an unconditional love.

Don't ever let me cause strife in their relationship. Make sure all my actions come from a heart of love and never from jealousy or hurt. Guard the words I speak, so they are only things that will build up their marriage.

Show me the special place I now have in my child's life. I know there is a new path ahead, and I pray I wouldn't walk it only looking backwards, wishing for the past.

Give me boundaries as I navigate, and help me never to insert myself between them. I love my child and his wife. Guide me as I look for ways to show them that love. Most of all, guard their marriage. Use every instance to pull them closer to You and closer to each other. Amen.

That is why a man leaves his father and mother and is united to his wife, and they become one flesh.

GENESIS 2:24 NIV

Help Me Love the Special Man in My Child's Life

God does not so much want us to do things
as to let people see what He can do.

A. B. SIMPSON

Dear Lord, my child has always been precious to me. I've held a unique place in her heart. As she grows and moves on, she's giving her heart to men. Help me know how to handle that. Truthfully, my first response is fear. I don't know these men, and I'm scared she'll be hurt by them.

I know I need to have more faith in her, and especially more faith in You. She has the foundation she needs to make wise choices about her heart. The problem is that I don't want to share her. Give her the godly insight she needs to continue to choose wisely.

She's so precious. How do I know she'll be treated right, especially now that she's away from home? Find ways to reassure me that she's okay. I need to know she's following You closely as she opens her heart to others.

As these men come into her life, help me view them not as competitors for her love, but as those who also love her. Remind me that they're here to continue my work as they protect and nurture her. Let me see them the way You do. Amen.

Submit to one another out of reverence for Christ.
EPHESIANS 5:21 NIV

Help Me Find Some Prayer Warriors

God has no greater controversy with His people today than this,
that with boundless promises to believing prayer, there are
so few who actually give themselves unto intercession.

A. T. PIERSON

Dear Lord, sometimes I think praying for my child is too big a job
for just one person. While he's away from home more and more,
help me find others who will band together with me to pray. I'm
asking for a group of people whom I can be real with. I don't want
the group to be just for me. I want us to come together for each
other.

Raising a child is so terrifying these days. Things we thought
were harmless, like sending them off to school and away on activities, are now fraught with hidden dangers. Lead me to others who
see what I see when I pray for the path that lies ahead of my child.

Develop in us the drive to pray for our kids. Help us hone
the insight that comes from Your Spirit so we know how to pray.
Then protect our time together so we have time to meet and pray
with one another. I know we can pray anytime, but I also know
the power that comes when we pray together.

Show me how to find such a
group. Bring unexpected people
into my life to populate this group.
Help me discern those You have
picked out for this group. Give each
of us confirmation about being part
of this group, and help us stay strong
and focused on You. Amen.

*"For where two or three
have gathered together in
My name, I am there
in their midst."*

MATTHEW 18:20 NASB

Help Us Present a United Front

Our love to God is measured by our everyday fellowship
with others and the love it displays.

ANDREW MURRAY

Dear Lord, so much of parenting is a partnership. I'm praying for my spouse and me to present a united front as we support our child. He's away from home more and more and testing his wings. We both have different opinions about what he's doing. Help us to disagree respectfully and in private.

Show us how to compromise when we make decisions without compromising our child's safety. Remind us to consult one another before we give an answer.

I know that my spouse wants only the best for our child, just like I do. But sometimes, in the heat of a disagreement, I let that truth escape my mind. Help me take a deep breath and work with my spouse as we navigate this new chapter in our child's life.

Don't let me disrespect my spouse in front of our child. Put a guard on my words before I can say something hurtful. Remind me that my spouse brings strengths to our parenting that I don't have. Help us both remember that we're stronger together than we are apart. Amen.

Teach a youth about the way he should go; even when he is old he will not depart from it.
PROVERBS 22:6 HCSB

Relish the Gift of Other Women in My Child's Life

{ *Be completely humble and gentle;*
be patient, bearing with one another in love.
EPHESIANS 4:2 NIV }

I've spent most of my adult life training my sons.

I—along with their father—had been preparing them to become men, independent and interdependent as they began dating and eventually chose wives. Seeing my sons dating was hard enough for me, but the choosing-wives part was something I had to work at. Truthfully, very few aspects of parenting came easily to me. Getting myself ready to turn them over to another woman was the hardest part.

Many women may think that having a family of men was difficult—not for me. I wasn't dismayed by being the only woman, I was delighted. I loved being the queen bee. My husband and sons spoiled me, and I relished their undivided attention.

Then the boys became teenagers and began to date. They brought girls into the house, and I found myself at a crossroads.

I remember one particular day so clearly. Our son had brought over a girl to hang out with us and watch a movie. She was a lovely girl, but obviously nervous. I was welcoming, but fairly quiet as I watched them interact with each other and with his father and me. My husband was perfect—just the right mix of polite banter and teasing that put her at ease. As she relaxed in our company, our son also relaxed.

That was the day I decided that I would treat each girl like she would one day become a vibrant part of our family. I didn't want any small thing early in their dating history to become a stumbling block between a future daughter-in-law and myself.

After that, I began to see these girls as allies, instead of competitors. They added a feminine point of view to my own in this house of men. I relished their company and rejoiced at what each added to our family, whether they became a permanent addition or not.

Iron Sharpens Iron

{ *As iron sharpens iron, so one person sharpens another.* }
PROVERBS 27:17 NIV

For anyone who has a child, the thought of perfect parenting elicits a range of emotions, from hope to discouragement to outright terror.

We all hope we'll be good parents, but most of us know we'll fall short in some ways. Every parent I've ever spoken with lives in fear of being such a bad parent that they scar their child permanently.

I'm writing this as I look back over my parenting journey. We have three grown sons, so the intense time of parenting is past. Sure, we still give advice—when asked—but for the most part, we're finished.

Looking back was scary at first. I was afraid of the regrets and remorse I'd feel from the perspective of what I know now. But the process of evaluation wasn't nearly as terror-inducing as I expected, because God gave me His perspective on my parenting journey. He showed me things I wouldn't have noticed if I'd been looking only through my own perspective. He reminded me that He wasn't like the animated stork that I'd seen in the Looney Tunes cartoons I watched on Saturday mornings growing up.

He *never* delivered the wrong baby to the wrong parents.

He chose my husband and me as parents for our boys before the beginning of time. He did it *knowing* the mistakes we'd make, as well as the parts we'd get right. He used us, for good and for bad, to help shape our kids as they grew. I'd never considered that perspective before—that God chose us as much for our weaknesses as parents as for our strengths. I'd never thought of this verse in the context of parenting before.

Does that absolve us of guilt where we've been wrong? Absolutely not. But it gives me confidence that God is true to His Word and will bring good out of bad. So when you are in the thick of parenting and struggling, remember that your child's future isn't in your hands. God's got this, and He always has.

Labels—Where Do Yours Come From?

{ *God paid a high price for you, so don't be enslaved by the world.* }
1 CORINTHIANS 7:23 NLT

We've all got them in our lives—people who are more than happy to label us. Sometimes the labels are good.

"You're a great parent."

"You're so smart."

"You're so beautiful."

"You're so organized . . .

"talented . . .

"spiritual . . .

"blessed."

These are the labels we like to hear—whether they're true or not. They have a seductive quality, inviting us to congratulate ourselves on what we've accomplished.

But sometimes the labels are bad.

"You're the worst parent ever."

"You're so selfish."

"You'll never amount to anything."

"You're such a liar . . .

"a betrayer . . .

"an untalented . . .

"hopeless."

Unlike the positive ones, these labels can devastate us. The echoes of these words take residence in our souls, providing a haunting refrain as we try to follow God's path. These labels get even more intense as our kids are away from home more and more. We judge our parenting skills on how well they do away from us, and the world is more than happy to help us do just that.

We can't get away from a world that seeks to define us, hanging labels on us for everyone to see. This is especially true when we're raising kids. The labels come from other parents, well-meaning bystanders, even our own children. Although we know we shouldn't, if we're not careful, we can begin to view ourselves through the filters of others.

But let's talk about labels from a manufacturing perspective. When goods are manufactured, there are only two sources that have the legal right to label them:

The one who manufactured the goods, and

The one who bought the goods.

That concept holds just as true for us as believers. Only two people have the authority and the right to label us:

The One who created us, and

The One who paid the ultimate price for our freedom.

Both of these also have labels for us.

"You are precious."

"You are loved."

"You are Mine."

It's time to banish the false labels—and the false labelers—from our minds, and focus on the only One who has the right to define us.

Develop Deep Roots

Man cannot be made secure by wickedness,
but the root of the righteous is immovable.
PROVERBS 12:3 HCSB

I remember a family trip when our boys were young. We'd traveled to Mississippi and been there when a tropical storm came onshore. We weren't hit by the brunt of it, although we did have a soggy weekend visiting grandparents. It began raining thirty minutes after we arrived and didn't stop until after we'd left to go back home. The drive back to South Carolina wasn't much fun, either.

We headed back up the interstate in the rain, and I couldn't help but notice numerous trees down on the side of the road. Although they were huge trees, it was obvious the damage hadn't come from high winds. But what else could have caused such a widespread calamity?

As I considered the soggy chaos, I realized the prolonged soaking rain held the answer. These particular trees, although still attached to large root-balls, hadn't developed the extended root system necessary to anchor them in near-flood conditions. Simply put, the rain had loosened the dirt, and without the root depth to hold them in place, they'd fallen to their deaths.

Studying the unfolding scene outside the car window led me to wonder about my own root system and the ones I was helping my boys develop. These tall trees had appeared strong and stable in normal conditions. But when stressed, they lacked the strength to survive. I thought I was doing everything I could to ensure their ability to weather a storm, but maybe it was time to take inventory.

It was up to me to stay faithful in parenting, so that when our boys were out in the world, they'd have the depth they needed to weather the storms that would come.

How About a Brother Night?

*By obedience to the truth, having purified yourselves
for sincere love of the brothers,
love one another
earnestly from a pure heart.*
1 PETER 1:22 HCSB

"Mom, can we have someone over to spend the night?" It had been a good week. Everyone's room was clean and all the chores were done. There really wasn't a good reason to deny the special privilege. Except one: I was exhausted. The thought of one, two, or three extra little bodies for the night made me want to curl up and cry. Then inspiration hit.

"How about a Brother Night instead?"

Three blank faces looked up at me.

"Brother Night?" I detected hopeful suspicion in the tone.

"Sure. It's just like when you have someone over. You stay up late, sleep in sleeping bags in the den, watch movies and eat popcorn. But it's just brothers."

"That's cool." The seal of approval from my ten-year-old made it official. Brother Night has been a tradition at our house ever since—even now that they're grown.

Brother Night has had a lot of benefits within our family. What started as an act of desperation, turned out to be pure inspiration. Now the physical distance between them doesn't matter. When they're back together, they look forward to some version of Brother Night. So often it's only when a fight comes up between siblings that parents emphasize how they should get along and be friends. Encouraging friendship outside of confrontation has allowed time for them to find things in common, things they liked to do together.

Don't try to walk the parenting road alone.

This looks different for each of us. We may be part of a solid marriage, where two parents generally agree. We may be part of a marriage where we have wildly different views of how to parent. We may be a single parent. Regardless of where we are personally, we still need others around us to help, especially when our child ventures outside of our home.

First and foremost, we must rely on God, knowing that He is always there with us. Beyond that, we need to reach out to others around us who can provide the support and encouragement we need. We'll find that this process isn't just for our benefit, but we'll also be helping others.

Life isn't just about me.

Being a parent is a selfless act. We sacrifice for our kids and frequently put ourselves second. But we have to be careful not to teach our kids that life is all about them. This is even harder when they're away from home.

It's a balancing act to show them how important they are to us, without making them think the world revolves around them.

Reaching out to others is important.

When we have more than one child, it's important to nurture their relationship with each other. After our oldest child left home, it was hard not to settle into the role of intermediary between him and his brothers. I had to consciously step back and force them to reach out to each other without my help.

I did have to remind them, but I didn't instigate the contact between brothers. As they made contacting each other a priority, it's stood them in good stead as they've grown. They each make an effort to stay in touch without relying on me.

Chapter Eight

My God, My Defender

Life is full of battles, many of which we're not equipped to fight alone. When we give our kids the assurance that God will always be their ultimate defender, we help them face anything that comes.

Protect My Child's Heart When Others Belittle Her

> Sometimes God allows what He hates
> to accomplish what He loves.
>
> JONI EARECKSON TADA

Dear Lord, You are supposed to be the only One we look to for affirmation. But this is easy to say and hard to do. Now that my child is away from my side more and more, I worry about how she'll react to criticism. Use the times when someone challenges her to draw her back to You for her self-worth and approval.

It's hard to move past the hurtful words of others, whether they're intended to hurt or instruct. Teach my child how to handle critical words. Remind her to turn to You when she's hurt. Put the pieces of her heart back together so that her ability to trust isn't damaged, and let her learn from what is said to her, regardless of the intent of the one who says it.

Don't let the harsh words of others permanently damage her tender heart. Use those difficult times to make her stronger. Let her experiences make her more aware of her own words and how they affect those around her.

She is infinitely precious to You. Remind her of this. Whisper Your own words of affirmation and love to her in the quietness of her soul. Amen.

The Lord will rescue me from every evil deed, and will bring me safely to His heavenly kingdom; to Him be the glory forever and ever. Amen.

2 TIMOTHY 4:18 NASB

Keep My Child Safe Every Night

Let God's promises shine on your problems.

CORRIE TEN BOOM

Dear Lord, please keep my child safe tonight, and every night that she's away. I'm so scared that she's not as safe as I imagine.

I know that You were always the One who watched over her, even when she was by my side. Continue to be her Protector, especially when she sleeps away from home.

Make sure she's warm and dry and has enough to eat. You are EL ROI, the God Who Watches. Give her proof that You are with her. Speak to her heart and reassure her. Gather her into Your arms and keep her safe, no matter how far she is from home.

Surround her with people who will guard her. Don't let anyone near who intends her harm. Give her insight into the motives and intentions of those she has chosen as companions. Amen.

She gave this name to the LORD who spoke to her: "You are the God who sees me," for she said, "I have now seen the One who sees me."

GENESIS 16:13 NIV

Keep My Child Safe Physically

Believers, look up—take courage.
The angels are nearer than you think.
BILLY GRAHAM

Dear Lord, my child is away from home right now. I can't see the situations he's encountering and it scares me. He has had the training he needs for this challenge, but I'm still fearful about his safety. What if he's attempting things that are dangerous? Things can happen unexpectedly, but I know that nothing ever catches You by surprise.

Put Your angels around him to guard him physically. Help him heed the insight You've provided to anticipate trouble. Make sure he listens to his instincts and listens to the still, small voice that speaks to his heart.

Give him the rest he needs to be refreshed and awake as he goes about his day. Don't let him be lulled into a false sense of security, feeling like nothing bad could ever happen to him. Keep his senses sharp and quick to catch the smallest whisper of danger.

Surround him with companions who can help him hone his skills and anticipate danger. I know he's exhilarated by this new opportunity, but don't let that blind him to the safety measures he needs to take. Show him how to enjoy life to the fullest while keeping his eyes open to the dangers that also come with these new experiences. Amen.

God is strong and can help you not to fall. He can bring you before his glory without any wrong in you and can give you great joy.

JUDE 24 NCV

Protect My Child from Bullying

I will not fear, for You are ever with me,
and You will never leave me to face my perils alone.

THOMAS MERTON

Dear Lord, I'm struggling because I can't protect my child. He's being bullied, and it's breaking my heart. I want to be there when it happens—to step between him and his attacker—but I can't. Please be his Protector.

I know the Bible tells us You have armies of angels. Send them to guard him from harm. Make sure he's safe physically and emotionally. I know that words can hurt us as badly as a physical assault.

Stand between him and the pain of these attacks. Don't let him be scarred emotionally or otherwise from what is happening now. Strike the hurt from his memory. Keep the pain from staying with him.

Don't let this make him turn in on himself. Instead, use this situation to open his eyes to how others can be hurt by words. Give him a kinder heart and empathy to anyone else who is being picked on.

Surround him with friends and champions who will take up for him. Use the words and actions of his friends to combat the attacks he's having to endure. Don't let those in authority over him ignore what's going on. Most of all, show him that You are always there with him. Amen.

"For the LORD your God is the one who goes with you to fight for you against your enemies to give you victory."

DEUTERONOMY 20:4 NIV

Protect My Child as She Travels by Car

Fear imprisons, faith liberates; fear paralyzes, faith empowers; fear disheartens, faith encourages; fear sickens, faith heals; fear makes useless, faith makes serviceable.

HARRY EMERSON FOSDICK

Dear Lord, when my child is traveling, I'm asking You to protect her. Make sure the vehicles that are transporting her are safe and well maintained. Don't let anything go wrong that could cause her, or those with her, to get hurt.

Make sure that whoever is driving is well rested. Don't let others in the car distract her. Give the driver focus and the ability to anticipate any upcoming danger.

Protect them from others who are on the road. Don't let another car veer into their path or have an issue that could lead to a collision. Make sure the road is free from debris and other dangers that could cause a wreck.

Help them to make wise decisions while they're traveling. It's so easy to get caught up in the moment. But I know that it only takes a second of lost concentration for catastrophe to strike.

You know everything, and are everywhere. Be with my child and those around her. Whisper insight and warnings to them when danger lies in their path. I know You love my child more than I can. Watch over her and hold her close. Amen.

To Him who led His people through the wilderness, for His lovingkindness is everlasting.

PSALM 136:16 NASB

Protect My Child as He Flies

If the Lord be with us, we have no cause of fear.
His eye is upon us, His arm over us, His ear open to
our prayer—His grace sufficient, His promise unchangeable.

JOHN NEWTON

Dear Lord, I'm excited that my child is getting to travel by plane. But I'm also fearful because, although it's rare, I know bad things can happen. Protect him so that he arrives safely at his destination.

Give the pilots the skill and insight they need to make good choices. Don't let any mechanical failure escape the notice of those inspecting the plane. Bring any anomaly to the attention of the ground crew before they get into the air.

I also worry about delays in his travel. Guide him and help him find his way. Don't let him get confused as he goes from one plane to another. Keep his luggage safe, and let it be there when he goes to pick it up.

Make his flight smooth, with little or no turbulence. Give him someone fun in the seat beside him. Don't let him sit beside someone who will make him uncomfortable.

As he travels, put people in his path to encourage him. Expand his way of looking at things. Bring to mind Your perspective as he views the world in a different way. Amen.

The LORD will protect your coming and going both now and forever.

PSALM 121:8 HCSB

Guard My Child's Tender Heart

Our lives are full of supposes. Suppose this should happen,
or suppose that should happen; what could we do; how could
we bear it? But if we are living in the high tower of the dwelling
place of God, all these supposes will drop out of our lives.
We shall be quiet from the fear of evil, for no threatenings
of evil can penetrate into the high tower of God.

HANNAH WHITALL SMITH

Dear Lord, my child has such a tender heart. Because of this, he's
so easily hurt. I can tell he views this as a weakness, but I know
You gave him this for a purpose. Show him what that purpose is.

As he grows, give him godly examples of others with tender
hearts and show him how that is an asset and not a liability. Don't
let him be ridiculed for caring. Let him see how his caring nature
can be used to encourage others. Provide him with the ability to
grow to his full potential.

Let him see the caring nature
of You, God. Help him recognize
Your love in himself. Protect him
from judging himself too harshly.
Show him that, as he embraces all
that You designed him to be, he's
glorifying You. Amen.

*He will cover you with His
feathers; you will take refuge
under His wings.
His faithfulness will be
a protective shield.*

PSALM 91:4 HCSB

Show My Child Your Power

Leave the broken, irreversible past in God's hands,
and step out into the invincible future with Him.

OSWALD CHAMBERS

Dear Lord, I'm afraid that as my child grows there'll be times when she's overwhelmed by circumstances. Without a focus on You, situations could get the better of her. She needs You to show her Your power and love.

She has a firm foundation of faith. Make sure she knows how to ride out the rough patches of life by holding on to You. When struggles come, do everything possible to encourage her to turn to You for help.

I know her faith needs to stretch and grow as she grows. But she also needs some confirmation of Your power to stand on. I'm so glad You're the One in charge of measuring out what each of us needs.

Help me be part of pointing her back to You when things fall apart. Don't let anything I say or do interfere with what You are doing in her life. Show us both how You're using this situation for good.

Help us both remember that You are worthy of our trust. Amen.

"The LORD is my strength and song, and He has become my salvation; this is my God, and I will praise Him; my father's God, and I will extol Him."

EXODUS 15:2 NASB

When Life Is Spiraling Out of Control

When we long for life without difficulties,
remind us that oaks grow strong in contrary winds,
and diamonds are made under pressure.

PETER MARSHALL

Dear Lord, You know how I feel right now. It seems like chaos is all around. Everywhere I turn, things are crumbling. My child is away from me right now, and I'm so scared about what might happen to him. I felt peace about letting him go, but now I only feel fear. Why are my emotions in chaos?

I feel lost and alone. I know in my head that You're close by, but my heart can't seem to sense You.

Renew my mind and help my emotions to fall in line. Take me to verses that speak of Your unwavering love and protection. Use others around me to remind me of Your steadfast love and care.

Most of all, protect my child. Protect him from anything that could happen. Keep him safe physically, and help us all to grow in our relationship with You. Amen.

And God is able to make all grace abound to you, so that always having all sufficiency in everything, you may have an abundance for every good deed.

2 CORINTHIANS 9:8 NASB

When Others Feed My Fear

> When a train goes through a tunnel and it gets dark,
> you don't throw away the ticket and jump off.
> You sit still and trust the engineer.
>
> CORRIE TEN BOOM

Dear Lord, I'm trying hard to be strong and focused on You, but the people around me seem to be working hard to keep me fearful. The more I try to focus on Your Word and avoid the fears that come into my mind about my child's safety and well-being, the more I get bombarded with what-ifs.

I know they are not trying to be hurtful, but their words are hurting me. The world is a scary place, even without people coming up with things to be fearful of. Help me know how to cope with this mess.

I want to protect myself, but I don't think lashing out is the best way to handle this. Am I angry because the fears aren't gone, but only hidden? I need to trust You even more. Help me answer them in love when they bring these difficult subjects up.

They're only voicing their own fears. Show me how to point them to You as the Author of peace. I need to remember Your faithfulness as I'm hit with unexpected missiles loaded with fear. You are Almighty God and there is nothing You can't do. Beyond that, You love our children more than we do. In Your hands is a safe place for them to rest. Amen.

The God of peace will soon crush Satan under your feet. The grace of our Lord Jesus be with you.

ROMANS 16:20 HCSB

When the Headlines Are Terrifying

> We fear men so much, because we fear God so little.
> One fear cures another. When man's terror scares you,
> turn your thoughts to the wrath of God.
>
> WILLIAM GURNALL

Dear Lord, the headlines today are terrifying, and I can't control my thoughts. They're rushing from what-if to what-if. All my child's life I've worked hard to protect her and provide a safe life for her. Now she's away from home more, and all I can think about is what could happen.

I don't have to use my imagination to envision horrifying scenarios. They're plastered in the headlines and on every type of media. Every day there are new ways that people have thought up to kill and injure our children.

Every time I see these things, my heart leaps toward my child. Show me how to conquer this monstrous fear. Inside I'm a knot of dreadful anticipation, waiting for tragedy to strike. This isn't the way You want me to live. Help me up out of this pit of despair.

Remind me of the ways You care for and protect my child. Show me how You've been strong even through tragedy. Don't let me dwell on circumstances that haven't even happened, but help me focus on You. You will be with us through everything, and that is my anchor. Amen.

*Some trust in chariots
and some in horses,
but we trust in the name
of the LORD our God.*
PSALM 20:7 NIV

Knowing I'm Not in This Alone

You need not cry very loud; he is nearer to us than we think.
BROTHER LAWRENCE

Dear Lord, as a parent I feel so alone, especially now that my child is away from home more often. She's facing so many things that I don't feel equipped to help her with. Remind me that You are here with me.

I need You so much right now. I want to be everything my child needs, but I can't. I'm not able to be with her every second of every day. I feel so inadequate when she shares things she's had to handle alone. I love that she asks for my advice, but what if I say the wrong thing and lead her astray?

Help me remember all the ways You've stood with me. I've never been alone in this, so why do I feel this way now?

It's the new things we're facing that have overwhelmed me with fear and doubt. Readjust my thinking and focus my thoughts upward. Bring Bible verses to my mind to help control my thoughts of failure and despair.

You are my strength. You have always stood strong with us, guiding me even when I didn't know it. I will continue to rely on You to give me whatever I need to help my child navigate this new chapter. Amen.

The LORD is near all who call out to Him, all who call out to Him with integrity. He fulfills the desires of those who fear Him; He hears their cry for help and saves them.

PSALM 145:18–19 HCSB

The Blessings of Following God

*For the LORD gives wisdom; from His mouth
come knowledge and understanding.*

PROVERBS 2:6 NASB

There have been many times in our sons' lives where they were more tuned in to God and His leading than I was. It shouldn't have surprised me, especially after the first few times, but it always did.

One of those times was when our youngest was in high school. He'd been playing baseball for years and had earned his way onto a travel ball team. As a left-handed pitcher, his goal was to eventually play on a college team. We supported him with lessons, carting him to and from practices, and arranging our schedules to travel with him when his team played.

The work was hard, requiring him to juggle baseball, school, and church activities. Achieving the goal he'd set for himself required more and more sacrifice, until he decided the price he was paying was too high.

His decision to quit seemed to come out of the blue. By the time he confided in us, I could see his decision had been made. "I just don't think I'm supposed to put sports over God." Who could argue with that, and who would want to? Truthfully, I'll admit I wanted to. I wanted him to have the opportunities that earning a spot—and possibly a scholarship—in college could give him. Beyond that, I confess that I loved sitting in the stands, the proud momma of a pitcher. In all the excitement and anticipation of the future, I had lost sight of the importance of his relationship with God here and now. I'm thankful he hadn't.

As he explained his thought process, I recognized how out of line I'd let my own priorities become. I gave him a big hug, and told him how proud I was of the decision he'd made. But this wasn't the end of the story.

Shortly after quitting baseball, he had the opportunity to take up tennis. He discovered his real gift as a tennis player and within six months was on the high school team. He went on to play tennis in college, and he got a position as a tennis coach at a summer camp where he worked.

Following God always leads to blessings, often in unexpected ways. When we allow God to be at the center of our parenting, we'll give our kids the foundation to make wise decisions with us and without us. It's a lesson I learned from watching my son.

Baggage or Luggage?

"Come to Me, all who are weary and heavy-laden, and I will give you rest. Take My yoke upon you and learn from Me, for I am gentle and humble in heart, and you will find rest for your souls. For My yoke is easy and My burden is light."
MATTHEW 11:28–30 NASB

I don't know about you, but I have trouble forgiving myself, especially when it comes to parenting mistakes. For some reason I expect a level of perfection from myself that I would never expect from someone else.

Because of this, I also struggle to accept God's forgiveness.

Somewhere deep inside is the fear that God has finally reached the limit of His patience with me and with my constant sin and shortcomings. Just writing this makes me shake my head because it's so far from the truth. But I'm sad to say, it's something I struggle with.

The result of this lack of forgiveness is that I carry a lot of baggage that I don't need to. I'm weighed down with past sins that God has long since forgiven. Even though I know God has been faithful to forgive, I still hesitate to return to Him over and over again, asking forgiveness for the same thing.

This also hinders me from following God's path when I'm making parenting decisions. I'm so weighed down with what might happen or how I might mess up, I find myself unable to move forward in faith. I make decisions hampered by baggage filled with fear and confusion about what to do.

That kind of thinking can weigh a person down.

Baggage is something I need to get rid of. I need to drop it at the feet of Jesus and leave it there.

Luggage, on the other hand, is something that equips us for our travels. My luggage consists of the things that God has blessed me with. It also includes the lessons I've learned through the struggles and the triumphs of walking with God.

It's the Bible verses I've memorized.

The praise songs that run through my mind.

The way I've seen God's faithfulness in my life and in the lives of my kids.

Everyone needs some luggage to be equipped for the parenting journey God has in store for us. The trick is to get rid of the baggage.

So today I ask you what I asked myself. Are you carrying parenting baggage or luggage on your journey?

Into the Storm

> As evening came, Jesus said to his disciples, "Let's cross to
> the other side of the lake." So they took Jesus in the boat
> and started out, leaving the crowds behind (although other
> boats followed). But soon a fierce storm came up. High waves
> were breaking into the boat, and it began to fill with water.
>
> MARK 4: 35–37 NLT

I've always known the storms of life would come. I also never believed that being a believer would guarantee me a life free from friction.

But I never clued in to the fact that sometimes being in the middle of God's perfect will would propel me into hurricane-force winds. It was in the middle of a tsunami-style parenting event that I went looking for confirmation that Jesus could—and would—calm the storm. What I found was that His plan was to be there with us through the storm.

Somehow I had developed the idea that God's will was a safe haven—a place without storms. I thought that when I was there, I'd be protected. Oh, I knew the enemy would throw the weight of his frustration against me, but I had this mistaken belief that God would direct me safely around and through his attacks.

During that particular storm, I saw something different as I studied this passage. It—and several others—show Jesus directing the disciples right into the teeth of danger. They obeyed, without the slightest hesitation, and ended up in the midst of chaos.

As I considered all the implications of this passage, it finally dawned on me that these storms have a purpose—a God-driven purpose. He sends us into these crazy-difficult situations to strengthen us and to give us a foundation for our faith. He does the same thing with our kids.

As parents, particularly when our kids are out of sight, those storms can appear out of nowhere. But we can face them with peace and confidence. Every time our boat seems swamped and danger surrounds us, He's there. He calms the waves of chaos when we turn to Him, each time making our faith stronger and more unshakable.

The One Who Really Keeps
My Child Safe

*And my God will supply all your needs according
to His riches in glory in Christ Jesus.*

PHILIPPIANS 4:19 NASB

The tendency of needing to always be in control caused me to spend a good part of my parenting years with an incorrect job description running through my head. Somehow, I'd gotten the idea that one of my primary goals as a parent was to protect my children. This was my responsibility, and it was up to me to make sure they stayed safe.

As my boys grew, this task became harder and harder. They were away from home more often, first at school, then sporting activities, and finally on their own driving and hanging out with friends. It just wasn't possible for me to anticipate everything that could happen and have safeguards in place to prevent catastrophe.

One night I came face-to-face with a brutal self-question. Could I really claim that I had kept my kids safe? Sure, I'd managed to help, but ultimately it hadn't been me. Had I taken on a task that wasn't mine?

While I wrestled with this new paradigm, I realized my thoughts were just another attempt at control. *I'd equipped . . . I'd given . . . I'd prevented.* In reality, I hadn't been the one to equip, give, or prevent. God had. Oh, He'd allowed me to help on occasion, but He'd been the One who'd orchestrated events to prepare my sons for life. It was a good thing too. I had no idea now where their lives were headed. I could make some guesses, but so far my track record wasn't good. But God's track record was perfect.

This verse in Philippians came immediately to mind, giving me comfort and peace. I could count on God's promises to be true not only in my life, but also in my children's lives.

Relyng on God

{
The LORD will protect you from all harm;
He will protect your life.
PSALM 121:7 HCSB
}

There have a been a lot of close calls during the growing years of our boys—and probably a lot more that I don't yet know about. But one that stands out in my mind happened when our youngest was still a baby. He was about sixteen weeks old that particular Christmas season, and we'd just put up our biggest Christmas tree ever. It was just over ten feet, a gorgeous fir tree, filled with glass balls, twinkling lights, and memories.

I'd carefully set the baby carrier, with our child strapped safely inside, on the couch and crossed the room to start the Christmas CDs. I turned back to the sofa just in time to watch the massive tree topple directly onto my child.

His wails began instantly, and I rushed to remove the tree, terrified of what I'd find. My mind had begun calculating the quickest routes to the hospital. But as I tossed the tree aside and began brushing glass from my newborn, panic turned to thanksgiving.

Although he was covered in glass and obviously scared, there wasn't a mark on him. Not a single scratch. I'd had experiences where God was there for me in the spiritual realm, and I knew that He could take care of me physically too. But that day, I saw how powerfully He could—and would—act when it came to keeping my child safe. Ever since, my faith has been much bolder and much stronger, knowing what it means to have Him watching over us, even when my sons are out of sight.

REMIND THEM THAT GOD IS THEIR ULTIMATE DEFENDER.

Chances are, you've already taught this before they left home, but it bears repeating. Just like praying first, remembering that God is in our corner can give even an impossible situation hope. Remind them of ways that God has been there for them. Share ways God has defended you. Always point them back to the One who can be there when you can't.

IDENTIFY THEIR GIFTS AND ENCOURAGE THEM.

God has made each of us unique. We all have gifts, and sometimes we're the last one to recognize our own. As parents, we have a good vantage point to help our child see the special abilities that God has given them, even when they're not at home. Sometimes the fact that they're away from us makes their strengths even more obvious.

Ask God to let you see your child through His eyes, and then let your kids know that you recognize their gifts. Positive reinforcement can provide the encouragement they need.

DON'T BE A LIST KEEPER.

When our kids are away from us, it's easy to get bogged down in negatives. Long-distance communication can be tricky, and it's easy for misunderstandings to crop up. It's up to us to let go of the hurts we may feel.

This isn't always easy to do, but we must remember the importance of keeping our relationship healthy. That's not possible if we're keeping a list of wrongs perpetrated against us.

Chapter Nine

Fully Present

It's easy to rush through life without savoring the blessings of the moments. It's our job as parents to help our kids develop the ability to live in the now, without wishing away their lives.

Surround My Child
with Encouragers

As we pour out our bitterness,
God pours in his peace.

F.B. MEYER

Dear Lord, as my child grows there are going to be times when it would be so easy for her to give in to self-doubt, fear, and frustration. Will You please surround her with people who have the gift of encouragement? Please help her to see that no matter what she's facing, You are right there with her.

Please bring her people with the right words and the right attitude for success. Give her good examples to follow. Let them speak truth to her in a way that she will receive it and grow from it. Make sure she has companions to encourage her faith. Bring people into her life who can help her see You in the midst of this difficult situation.

I know You are there with her, sometimes standing beside her, sometimes in front of her, and sometimes carrying her. Let her feel Your comfort and peace, especially when hard times come.

Give her hope where there seems to be no hope. Show her joy when circumstances dictate otherwise. Most of all, equip her with Your strength to stay strong and faithful. Amen.

Don't say, "I will avenge this evil!" Wait on the LORD, and He will rescue you.

PROVERBS 20:22 HCSB

Teach My Child How to Trust

> If we cannot believe God when circumstances
> seem be against us, we do not believe Him at all.
>
> CHARLES SPURGEON

Dear Lord, I know that sometimes trusting means getting hurt. Show my child You are trustworthy by bringing people into his life who are trustworthy.

Give him true friends who won't betray him, and companions who will help build up his heart. Remind him that there are good people in the world. Don't let his heart get hardened.

Please bring people into his life that will encourage that sense of trust. Let them be examples of integrity whom he can follow.

Guide him so that he makes wise choices about whom to trust. Give him a spirit of discernment to place that trust carefully and wisely.

Surround him with advisers, colleagues, and friends who share his values and character. Let them be a living reminder that it's important to be trustworthy. Most of all, remind him that no matter what, You are worthy of his trust. Amen.

> *Trust in the LORD with all your heart and do not lean on your own understanding.*
>
> PROVERBS 3:5 NASB

Help My Child Focus on Her Studies

The humblest occupation has in it materials
of discipline for the highest heaven.
FREDERICK W. ROBERTSON

Dear Lord, my child is having so much fun as she launches into a new chapter of her life. But I worry she'll let fun come between her and the purpose she has. As she's away from home more and more, remind her to keep her priorities grounded. Don't let her neglect her studies.

I know how easy it is to get sidetracked when everything is new and exciting. Guard her mind and give her the focus she needs to keep up her grades. I'm praying that these new experiences help her grow as she learns how to balance her life.

Give her good friends to spend time with. Make sure they also have solid priorities and aren't those who chase only after excitement. As she explores and expands her horizon, make sure she listens to Your Spirit. I want her to experience new things, but not at the expense of compromising her character and her priorities.

Help her have encouraging instructors who see her gifts and abilities clearly. Don't let those in authority over her discourage her. Instead, may they help her grow with gentle insight. Most of all, make sure she sees herself and her abilities only through Your eyes. Amen.

*The mind of the prudent
acquires knowledge,
and the ear of the wise
seeks knowledge.*
PROVERBS 18:15 NASB

Make My Child Uncomfortable

> Comfort and prosperity have never enriched
> the world as much as adversity has.
> BILLY GRAHAM

Dear Lord, my child is in a place that's far from home and even farther from You. She's comfortable with her situation and doesn't see the immediate need for You. I'm asking You to step in and make her uncomfortable.

My soul quakes as I whisper this dangerous prayer. I don't want bad things to happen to her. But when she makes bad choices, help her to know that, to perceive the consequences before it is too late to make a change.

Give her the wake-up call she needs.

Please protect her as You shake her up. Give those she trusts and respects the godly wisdom to weigh in about her choices and how she's navigating her life. Don't let her be influenced by those who don't know You.

Guard her now for the long term, instead of just the short term. Use any upheaval to pull her back into Your loving arms. Don't let any past hurts from people stand between her and a renewed relationship with You. Most of all, don't let her go far away from You. Amen.

> *"As many as I love,*
> *I rebuke and discipline.*
> *So be committed and repent."*
> REVELATION 3:19 HCSB

Show My Child How to Choose Joy

Your success and happiness lies in you.
Resolve to keep happy, and your joy and you shall form
an invincible host against difficulties.

HELEN KELLER

Dear Lord, as my child grows he's going to go through times of hopelessness. When those struggles come, don't let him get so bogged down in circumstances it affects his attitude. Show him how to hold on to his joy in spite of difficulties.

Draw him even closer to You when these times come. Make him hungry for You and for reading the Bible. I know how spending time reading Your Word makes such a difference in my life. Give him the same experience. So often we look for complicated answers when the truth is as simple as opening a book.

Use these times to teach him that joy isn't dependent on circumstances. Our joy comes from You, and there are no circumstances too big for You. Help him learn this lesson early.

Surround him with others who can share this truth. Give them insight about what he needs to hear from them, and how they can help him adjust his attitude. Remind him that nothing is too big or too small for You. Amen.

Now may the God of hope fill you with all joy and peace in believing, so that you will abound in hope by the power of the Holy Spirit.

ROMANS 15:13 NASB

Help My Child Love Those Who Are Different

None are more unjust in their judgments of others
than those who have a high opinion of themselves.
CHARLES SPURGEON

Dear Lord, as my child is away from home more, she's being exposed to people who are very different from her. I'm praying that she won't judge others by what she sees on the surface.

Show her how to give each one a chance to reveal what's inside before she jumps to judgment. Remind her that it's not the clothes or skin color or even the way people talk that determines who they are. Give her the wisdom she needs as she chooses friends from the inside out.

Help her develop her insight about others and view them only through Your eyes.

Remind her that many people hide behind a public mask. They protect themselves by wearing odd things or acting in ways that may not be appropriate. Let her reach out in love to those You put in her path. Amen.

*So God created mankind
in his own image,
in the image of God
he created them; male and
female he created them.*
GENESIS 1:27 NIV

Give Me Your Perspective about My Child's Life

The remedy for discouragement is the Word of God.
When you feed your heart and mind with its truth,
you regain your perspective and find renewed strength.

WARREN WIERSBE

Dear Lord, I get so wrapped up in the here and now that I lose perspective, especially when it comes to my child. Give me a glimpse of Your view for his life. Everything he's experiencing right now seems so urgent. Show me how the difficulties he's facing will help him grow into the man You have ordained him to be.

You see everything from a view that I cannot have. But I know You can give me a hint of how You're working through the situation he's in. Bring Bible verses to my mind that reinforce how much You love him and how You will never abandon him.

Remind me of the ways You've worked through the difficulties in my own life to bring about blessings. I know that You are a God who blesses. Show me that truth in the circumstances of my child's life.

As I pray for him, give me a sense of peace that my words are reaching Your ears, especially when my prayers don't feel powerful. Help me to stop relying on how I feel to gauge Your level of work in his life. You work in ways I cannot see, but I'm choosing to trust You even when it appears that nothing is happening. Amen.

Now faith is confidence in what we hope for and assurance about what we do not see.

HEBREWS 11:1 NIV

Help Me to Balance My Life

The fear of man strangles us, because we can never
please everybody; but the fear of the Lord frees us, because
it challenges us to live and serve for an audience of One.

PAUL CHAPPELL

Dear Lord, I'm caught between my child and my parents. I thought this time of life, when my child was leaving home for the first time, would mean freedom and the ability to be an active part of his life. Instead, I'm caught between caring for my aging parents and him. They all need me. Show me how to prioritize my life.

Every day I feel like I'm neglecting someone. I'm exhausted and frustrated. Instead of finding joy in this new chapter, I just want to hide from a situation that asks more than I'm able to supply.

Surround me with others who have been where I am. Let me see their victories so I can learn and follow in their footsteps. Keep my child and my parents from resenting me and my choices.

I need Your strength as I learn how to walk this treacherous path. I admit that I am not up to this task. If I try to do this by myself, I have no hope. Remind me that You are everything I need to make it through victorious. Amen.

> "Behold, I am the LORD, the God of all flesh; is anything too difficult for Me?"
>
> JEREMIAH 32:27 NASB

Help Me Set Healthy Boundaries

When God speaks, oftentimes His voice
will call for an act of courage on our part.
CHARLES STANLEY

Dear Lord, now that my child is away from home more, help me to set healthy boundaries, for her and for me. I have raised her in Your Word and surrounded by Your truth. Help me to trust her and You as she learns how to live her own life.

I respect her right to make these choices, even if I don't agree with them. Help me to be a bridge and an example of Your love. Help me to maintain my own standards, even when she challenges or disregards my position, but without alienating her. Give me the strength I need to remain steadfast, even when my precious child disagrees.

Help her understand my choices. Don't let her feel that my love is conditional. It's not. I will always love her, and it has nothing to do with what she does or doesn't do. But just as she is determining who she will be and how she will act, I have to do the same.

Show me how to set these boundaries in a healthy way. There are difficult conversations ahead of me, and I need Your words instead of my own. I know this isn't something I can accomplish in my own strength. Walk before me and show me how to work this out. Amen.

*Be on your guard; stand firm
in the faith; be courageous;
be strong.*
1 CORINTHIANS 16:13 NIV

Don't Let Me Neglect the Ones Still at Home

Faith consists, not in ignorance, but in knowledge,
and that, not only of God, but also of the divine will.

JOHN CALVIN

Dear Lord, while my child is away don't let me neglect those still at home. I know I'm expending a lot of energy thinking and worrying about her while she's gone. I still have others here who need me to be present in their lives.

Having a child away from home is different than I thought it would be. I'm more consumed by fear and worry than I expected. Don't let those here at home think I love them any less.

I want my child to know how much she's missed. I want to include her as much as possible. Please remind me not to do that at the expense of those close by. I need to find the right balance for this new family path.

I need to readjust my focus on You, instead of the one who's far away. When I keep my eyes firmly fixed upward, You can direct my thoughts and actions to the child who needs me right now, no matter how close or far they are. Without Your guidance, I'm struggling in my own strength and I know that's never enough. Amen.

Fathers, do not exasperate your children; instead, bring them up in the training and instruction of the Lord.

EPHESIANS 6:4 NIV

The Myth of Perfect Parenting

{
I want to do what is good, but I don't.
I don't want to do what is wrong, but I do it anyway.
ROMANS 7:19 NLT
}

Coming into this parenting journey, my goal was to be perfect. Or at least I wanted to be as perfect as possible. I didn't want anything I did—or didn't do—to affect my kids negatively. It didn't take long to figure out this wasn't going to happen.

I remember one time in particular when I had the best of intentions. Our oldest child was born picky. He had certain likes and dislikes and nothing we tried to do could change them. One of the things he did *not* like was getting dirty, especially getting his hands dirty. This quirk even affected what foods he ate and how he ate it. As a toddler, he refused to pick up any food that would get his hands dirty. This even extended to an aversion of handling things that had crumbs—like crackers and cookies.

This particular day I decided the time had come to introduce him to the fun that could be had by getting his hands dirty. I thought baking cookies would be the perfect way to sneak him into using his hands. I choose a recipe for sugar cookies that required working with the dough and getting messy.

He was fine with helping add the ingredients to the bowl to mix, but when it came time to sprinkle the counter with flour so we could roll out the dough he balked. No way was he putting flour on his hands. In an effort to get him to loosen up, I flicked flour on myself to show him getting dirty was fun. He laughed, so I thought I'd take it one step further and flicked flour on him.

Instead of more laughter, my act was met with howls of anguish as he fled the room. He barricaded himself in the bathroom until I promised no more baking. Definitely not one of my best momma moments.

Eventually he did lose his aversion to getting dirty, but it wasn't anything I could take credit for. He grew out of it naturally.

Perfect parents don't guarantee perfect kids. Whether the mistakes we make happen when they're with us, or when they're away from us, God can and will affect the outcome. I could have done every single thing right as a mother, and because of free will, any of my sons could have chosen the wrong path. How do I know this is true? Because God is perfect, and look how we turned out. He did everything right, but we still chose to go our own way.

The Power of Transparency

"He must increase, but I must decrease."

JOHN 3:30 NASB

As difficult as parenting is these days, I believe it's even harder to be a child growing up. There are so many temptations that we, as parents, didn't have to face. Early on, I tried to help guide them by giving them a standard to live up to—me. But it didn't take me long to realize that setting myself up as a strong example carried some wicked pitfalls.

First, I was far from perfect. Using myself as an ideal meant I had to be good most of the time. I realized early on that wasn't going to happen. Sometimes I get it right, but a lot of the time, I don't.

Second, because I wasn't perfect, and was trying to set a good example, I found myself justifying my flaws and minimizing my mistakes. That was the exact opposite of how I wanted them to go through life. Thank goodness God stepped in and helped me see what I needed to do.

I learned that what I had to do was practice transparency with my kids. That means I had to draw a clear contrast between the mess God has to work through (that would be me) and the results of His miraculous effort. But for this strategy to be effective I have to be willing to show myself honestly—with all my flaws.

At first it was as scary as the whole becoming-a-parent thing.

But after a time or two of letting my boys see through the me I wished I was—and tried to pretend to be—and directly at who I actually was, I discovered something.

There truly is an amazing freedom in just being yourself. I no longer had to keep up the pretense of being spiritual or an expert or anything else. Instead, I could just relax and *be*—resting in whatever God wanted to bring out.

This transparency also took the pressure off my kids. They weren't misled into believing they had to be something they weren't. They didn't have to start out already *good enough* to qualify to get better. They could start right were they were. This lesson stood them in good stead as they interacted with life away from home.

Finally, it brought the added benefit of making me a safe person to share their struggles with. By being real, I gave them the freedom to discuss things that happened away from home with me.

Learning this lesson has led to some pretty amazing conversations. It was hard, but learning to let them see me struggle gave them permission to face life and all its messiness.

Thankful for Today

{
Be silent before the LORD and wait expectantly for Him;
do not be agitated by one who prospers in his way,
by the man who carries out evil plans.
}

PSALM 37:7 HCSB

Parenting isn't a job for sissies. Being entrusted with the life of someone else—even for a short time—is a scary proposition. Beyond that, those we're entrusted with don't always appreciate how hard the job is. Sometimes they even appear to go out of their way to make it harder.

I've found there's a lot of patience required in parenting. I don't know about you, but waiting patiently and appreciating the journey isn't really my gift. I hate being patient; whatever it is—I want it, and I want it now. I would like to think I'm a product of my times and environment. After all, we live in a world of the instant now.

Going along with my lack of patience is the fact that being thankful for today wasn't always something I excelled at. When our sons were young, I often found myself impatient for the milestones to come—when they were potty trained, when they could talk, when they could drive. Then one day my husband turned to me and said the words that would change my perspective forever.

"Quit wishing away their lives. We only have them a short time, let's enjoy *every* moment, not just the easy ones."

Ouch. In two short sentences, he'd rocked my world. The truth of what I'd been doing hit me like an arrow to the heart. Instead of finding joy in the moments, I had fallen into the trap of always wishing we were at a different place.

It's been a tough lesson, but I've learned that fast-forwarding through life isn't a shortcut to happiness. There is joy in every moment of our lives if we just look for it and learn to be thankful for today. I've even learned not to wish them back home sooner when they're away. God has lessons for them to learn away from us. I don't ever want to stand between my kids and God.

Spending Time

{ *But if we walk in the light as He Himself is in the light,*
we have fellowship with one another,
and the blood of Jesus His Son cleanses us from all sin. }

1 JOHN 1:7 HCSB

My husband and I have always been outspoken parents who try to be friends instead of . . . well . . . parents. But this has never interfered with having fun with the boys. I remember one winter, soon after we'd moved to South Carolina, we got hit with thirteen-plus inches of snow (not a normal occurrence).

This snow inspired them to turn their skateboards into snowboards. It actually worked pretty well. The lot our house is built on slopes down away from the street and it made a perfect fifty-foot slope, and—if you didn't count the inherent danger of falling—it was relatively safe.

The boys had been joined by a gang of friends from the neighborhood. Several moms had also dropped by to check on the goings-on as well. As each one came, she was immediately besieged by requests to join in the fun. I watched as each mother intelligently declined the invitation. I also watched the disappointment on the young faces.

They'd worked so hard and were having so much fun they really wanted a grown-up to share the experience. I'd like to say I was moved by all the sad faces and didn't want my sons to be disappointed. Honesty compels me to confess that was only part of my reason. I'm also a daredevil at heart.

So when they invited me, I didn't hesitate. I'm sure I looked like a moving windmill as I rode down the hill, but all I could hear were the joyful yells of three proud children.

This time it happened while they were at home, but I've also been called on when they were far away. I've learned never to let dignity and what others think stand in the way of participating in my kids' lives.

SHARE THEIR LIVES.

Kids go through a lot of emotions when they're away from home—some reasonable, some not. One of the things they struggle with is feeling less important because they're not with you all the time. We can combat that by making sharing their lives a priority. We can't always do life together in person, but we can take an interest in what interests them.

BE AVAILABLE ON THEIR TIME FRAME.

I had to develop a sort of parenting radar that would alert me to the fact that one of my boys needed to talk, especially when we were in different places and the conversations took place on the phone or video chat. The beginning of the conversations tended to be offhand and it was easy to miss the fact that what was coming was important. It took practice. I can tell you from experience, those times were rarely convenient, but they were *always* important.

Looking back, I regret not stopping more and being available when they asked. I don't have a single regret about the times I cancelled appointments or stayed up late to spend time with them.

DON'T BE PREDICTABLE.

Consistency is good—predictability isn't. It's easy to get in a rut when our kids aren't home. We call them at a certain time every week, ask about the same things, talk the same amount of time. This isn't a good thing: it's a boring thing.

Instead look for new ways to communicate, new things

223

to share. Send pictures or even videos to your kids. If you normally connect through a phone call, instead plan a video chat. With smartphones we can even include them at events they might otherwise miss.

Acknowledgments

No book can ever see the light of day without an entire team of people moving it forward. That's especially true of this book!

First and foremost, I want to give a shout-out to my long-suffering husband, Kirk Melson. Without his willingness to chip in with almost everything around the house, this book would never have happened.

I also want to thank those in my life who have given this project, and all of us involved, much-needed—daily—prayer support: Cathy Baker, Candace Brady, Emme Gannon, Kathy Garrett, Noelle Lawson, Paula Mauer, Sandy Dewitt, Sheri Owens, Sherri Jones, Tara Allen, Tarah Smith, Valorie Moore, and Vonda Skelton. I could never leave out my precious critique group with Lynette Eason, Alycia Morales, and Mary Denman.

A special shout-out goes to my amazing (and, in my opinion, the best) agent in the world, David Van Diest.

Of course I want to include everyone at Worthy Inspired. You are the greatest group any author could ever hope to be blessed with. Thank you, Pamela Clements, for believing in me and for the work and support of the entire Worthy team.

Additionally, no writer is ever able to move ahead without other writers to share the journey! Thank you to all the writers from Cross N Pens, ACFW SC Chapter, My Book Therapy, and of course the Light Brigade.

I want to also give a shout-out to my extended family, my sister and family—Katy, Kurt, and Ellery Schneider. Finally, I could never neglect to mention my parents, Jim and Monita Mahoney. You all have always believed in me and been among my staunchest supporters.

About the Author

Edie Melson is an author, blogger, and speaker who has a passion to share what the love of God looks like in practical application. Her heart to help others hear from God and find His path for their lives has connected her with women all over the country. She has penned numerous books, including *While My Soldier Serves*, a book of prayers for those with a loved one in the military. As a sought-after speaker, she's encouraged and challenged audiences in person and online. She's also the military family blogger at Guideposts.org and monthly columnist at PuttingOnTheNew.com. She and husband Kirk have been married thirty-five years and raised three sons. They live in Simpsonville, South Carolina.

Visit Edie on her website, www.EdieMelson.com

IF YOU ENJOYED THIS BOOK, WILL YOU CONSIDER SHARING THE MESSAGE WITH OTHERS?

Mention the book in a blog post or through Facebook, Twitter, Pinterest, or upload a picture through Instagram.

Recommend this book to those in your small group, book club, workplace, and classes.

Head over to facebook.com/worthypublishing, "LIKE" the page, and post a comment as to what you enjoyed the most.

Tweet "I recommend reading #WhileMyChildIsAway by @EdieMelson // @worthypub"

Pick up a copy for someone you know who would be challenged and encouraged by this message.

Write a book review online.

Visit us at worthypublishing.com

twitter.com/worthypub

worthypub.tumblr.com

facebook.com/worthypublishing

pinterest.com/worthypub

instagram.com/worthypub

youtube.com/worthypublishing